CCSS Prep
Grade 3
Editing and Revising

by Dana Konopka and Suzanne Borner

Edited by Patricia F. Braccio and Ralph R. Kantrowitz

Item Code: RAS 2707• Copyright © 2013 Queue, Inc.

Queue, Inc. • 80 Hathaway Drive, Stratford, CT 06615
(800) 232-2224 • Fax: (800) 775-2729 • www.qworkbooks.com

TABLE OF CONTENTS

TO THE STUDENTS

In this editing and revising workbook, you will read many passages. You will then answer multiple-choice questions about what you have read.

As you read and answer the questions, please remember:

- You may refer back to the passage as often as you like.

- Read each question very carefully and choose the **best** answer.

- Indicate the correct multiple-choice answers directly in this workbook. Circle or underline the correct answer.

- Remember what you know about correct grammar, punctuation, and English usage.

iv

Nate is in the third grade. His class is learning how to write stories. His teacher asked each student to remember a time when he or she did a good thing and to write a story telling about that time. Nate planned his story and wrote his rough draft. Now he needs your help editing and revising it.

Here is Nate's rough draft. Read it and then answer questions 1–10.

(1) Yesterday, on <u>January 15 2009,</u> I felt very good because I did the right thing. (2) I went out to the bus stop to wait for the school bus. (3) It was early in the morning. (4) It felt like <u>the most cold day</u> of the year. (5) I was the first one to get to the bus stop. (6) The other kids got there after a while, and <u>they ask me</u> if I was going to cross the street. (7) I said, "No, we are not supposed to cross the street." (8) They laughed at me, and then I felt embarrassed. (9) The other kids all walked across the street. (10) That is a dangerous thing to do. (11) It is really dangerous because you could get hit by a car. (12) Because is a very busy street! (13) We are supposed to wait for that our bus to come before we cross the street.

(14) When the bus came, the other kids got on first because I still had to cross the street. (15) I waited for <u>the bus driver's nod.</u> (16) I felt proud when the bus driver said, "Good job. (17) You waited where you were supposed to wait." (18) I felt proud because I did <u>sumthing</u> good and I did not let those kids make me change my mind. (19) One time at school I also felt proud because I won an award for attendance.

1. Choose the correct way to write the underlined part of sentence 1.

   Yesterday, on <u>January 15 2009,</u> I felt very good because I did the right thing.

   a. january 15 2009,
   b. January 15, 2009,
   c. January, 15, 2009,
   d. No change is needed.

2. Which one of these is **not** a complete sentence?

    f. I said, "No, we are not supposed to cross the street."
    g. That is a dangerous thing to do.
    h. Because is a very busy street!
    j. I waited for the bus driver's nod.

3. Choose the correct way to write the underlined part of sentence 4.

    It felt like <u>the most cold day</u> of the year.

    a. the mostest cold day
    b. the colder day
    c. the coldest day
    d. No change is needed.

4. Read sentence 13. It is poorly written.

    We are supposed to wait for that our bus to come before we cross the street.

    Choose the **best** way to rewrite this sentence.

    f. We are supposed to wait for our bus to come before we cross the street.
    g. We are supposed to wait for when our bus to come before we cross the street.
    h. We are supposed to wait for where our bus to come before we cross the street.
    j. We supposed to wait for our bus to come before we cross the street.

5. Choose the correct way to write the underlined part of sentence 6.

The other kids got there after a while, and <u>they ask me</u> if I was going to cross the street.

   a. they asked me
   b. they will ask me
   c. they asking me
   d. No change is needed.

6. Choose the **best** way to combine the ideas in sentences 10 and 11 into one sentence.

That is a dangerous thing to do. It is really dangerous because you could get hit by a car.

   f. Getting hit by a car is a dangerous thing to do.
   g. That is a dangerous thing because you could get hit by a car.
   h. That is a dangerous thing, dangerous because you could get hit by a car.
   j. That is a danger to cars that hit.

7. Choose the correct way to write the underlined part of sentence 15.

I waited for <u>the bus driver's nod.</u>

   a. the bus drivers nod.
   b. the bus drivers' nod.
   c. the bus drivers's nod.
   d. No change is needed.

8. Choose the sentence that does **not** belong in the paragraph that begins with sentence 14.

    f. sentence 14
    g. sentence 15
    h. sentence 19
    j. sentence 16

9. Choose the correct way to write the underlined part of sentence 18.

    I felt proud because I did <u>sumthing</u> good and I did not let those kids make me change my mind.

    a. somthing
    b. something
    c. sommething
    d. No change is needed.

10. Nate wants to add this sentence to the paragraph that begins with sentence 14.

    I couldn't wait to tell my parents.

    Where would the sentence **best** fit?

    f. right after sentence 16
    g. right after sentence 14
    h. right after sentence 18
    j. right after sentence 19

4

Matt is in the third grade. His class is learning how to write thank-you letters. Matt decided to write a letter to his grandmother. He wanted to thank her for taking him to the nature center last Saturday. Matt wrote a rough draft of his letter. Now he needs your help editing and revising it.

Here is Matt's rough draft. Read it and then answer questions 1–10.

(1) Dear grandma,

    (2) Thank you very much for taking me to the nature center last Saturday it was really fun. (3) I enjoyed <u>the hiking trails better.</u>

    (4) The hiking trails <u>be fun.</u> (5) I loved walking along the Appalachian Trail. (6) We could have walked all the way to Maine! (7) I can't believe Uncle Bill hiked the whole trail. (8) That's more than 2,000 miles! (9) When I grow up, I want to hike all the way <u>from Georgia to Maine, to.</u> (10) When I grow up, I would like to hike it all.

    (11) Inside the nature center, I liked the microscope. (12) I used it to look at rocks and feathers. (13) From the moon was one of the rocks! (14) I looked at <u>feathers from an eagle a parrot a sea gull.</u>

    (15) Thanks again, Grandma. (16) I hope I can come visit you again soon.

                       (17) Love,

                       (18) Matt

1. Choose the correct way to write line 1, the opening of the letter.

   Dear grandma,

   a. dear grandma,
   b. Deer grandma,
   c. Dear Grandma,
   d. No change is needed.

2. Choose the sentence that **best** fits right after sentence 12.

    f. Maybe Uncle Bill would like to come with me.
    g. Eagles are beautiful.
    h. I had never used a microscope before.
    j. Hiking is a lot of fun, but it's also hard work.

3. Read sentence 2. It is poorly written.

Thank you very much for taking me to the nature center last Saturday it was really fun.

Choose the **best** way to rewrite this sentence.

    a. Thank you very much for taking me to the nature center last Saturday It was really fun.
    b. Thank you very much for taking me to the nature center last Saturday was really fun.
    c. Thank you very much for taking me to the nature center last Saturday. It was really fun.
    d. Thank you for the last Saturday nature center.

4. Choose the correct way to write the underlined part of sentence 3.

    I enjoyed <u>the hiking trails better.</u>

    f. the hiking trails most of all.
    g. the hiking trails more better.
    h. the hiking trails bestest.
    j. No change is needed.

6

5. Choose the correct way to write the underlined part of sentence 4.

The hiking trails <u>be fun.</u>

   a. was fun.
   b. were fun.
   c. is fun.
   d. No change is needed.

6. Read sentence 13. It is poorly written.

From the moon was one of the rocks!

Choose the **best** way to rewrite this sentence.

   f. The moon had one of the rocks!
   g. One of the rocks was from the moon!
   h. One was moon rock!
   j. One of the rocks was on the moon!

7. Choose the correct way to write the underlined part of sentence 9.

When I grow up, I want to hike all the way <u>from Georgia to Maine, to.</u>

   a. from Georgia to Maine, two.
   b. from Georgia to Maine, though.
   c. from Georgia to Maine, too.
   d. No change is needed.

8. Choose the **best** way to combine the ideas in sentences 9 and 10 into one sentence.

> **When I grow up, I want to hike all the way <u>from Georgia to Maine, to.</u> When I grow up, I would like to hike it all.**

   f. When I grow up, I also want to hike all the way from Georgia to Maine.

   g. I want to grow up and hike all the way from Georgia to Maine.

   h. When I grow up, I want to hike.

   j. When I hike all the way from Georgia to Maine, I will grow up.

9. Choose the correct way to write the underlined part of sentence 14.

> **I looked at <u>feathers from an eagle a parrot a sea gull.</u>**

   a. feathers from an eagle, a parrot, and a sea gull.

   b. feathers from an eagle a parrot, and, a sea gull.

   c. feathers from an eagle, a parrot, a sea gull.

   d. No change is needed.

10. Matt wants to add this sentence either to the paragraph that begins with sentence 11 or the paragraph that begins with sentence 15.

> **Could we please go to the nature center again?**

Where would the sentence **best** fit?

   f. right after sentence 13

   g. right after sentence 14

   h. right after sentence 11

   j. right after sentence 16

David is in the third grade. His class is learning about recycling. His teacher asked the students to write about what they do to recycle. David made a list of his ideas, and then he wrote a rough draft. Now he needs your help editing and revising it.

Here is David's rough draft. Read it and then answer questions 1–10.

(1) Recycling is important. (2) <u>Everbody</u> should recycle. (3) If they did, there would be less waste in our landfills. (4) Our landfills would be smaller.

(5) There are a few things I do at my house. (6) To recycle. (7) I put <u>all of the Newspapers</u> into brown paper bags. (8) Sometimes we have to ask for <u>an paper bag</u> at the grocery store. (9) Otherwise they just give us plastic. (10) I rinse out all the cans that we use. (11) <u>I put it in a special container</u> that we keep in the garage. (12) I do the same thing with glass jars. (13) The cans and jars <u>went</u> in the same big box. (14) We have so many boxes from when we moved in last year.

(15) Every Tuesday we put out the garbage. (16) <u>The recycling box go</u> next to the garbage. (17) The papers get stacked on top. (18) It's that simple!

1. Choose the correct way to write the underlined part of sentence 2.

   <u>Everbody</u> should recycle.

   a. Everybuddy
   b. evrybody
   c. Everybody
   d. No change is needed.

2. Choose the **best** way to combine the ideas in sentences 3 and 4 into one sentence.

   If they did, there would be less waste in our landfills. Our landfills would be smaller.

   f. Our landfills would be smaller because there would be less waste.
   g. There would be smaller waste in our landfills.
   h. There would be less small waste in our landfills.
   j. There would be landfills that are smaller.

3. Choose the correct way to write the underlined part of sentence 7.

I put <u>all of the Newspapers</u> into brown paper bags.

   a. all of the Newspaper
   b. all of The Newspapers
   c. all of the newspapers
   d. No change is needed.

4. Which one of these is **not** a complete sentence?

   f. Everybody should recycle.
   g. To recycle.
   h. Otherwise they just give us plastic.
   j. The papers get stacked up.

5. Choose the correct way to write the underlined part of sentence 8.

Sometimes we have to ask for <u>an paper bag</u> at the grocery store.

   a. a paper bag
   b. an papered bag
   c. an paper bags
   d. No change is needed.

6. Choose the **best** way to combine the ideas in sentences 5 and 6 into one sentence.

There are a few things I do at my house. To recycle.

   f. I recycle a few things at my house.
   g. There are a few things I do to recycle my house.
   h. There are a few things I do at my house to recycle.
   j. There are a few things at my house to recycle.

7. Choose the correct way to write the underlined part of sentence 11.

   <u>I put it in a special container</u> that we keep in the garage.

   a. I put him in a special container
   b. I put them in a special container
   c. I put in a special container
   d. No change is needed.

8. Choose the correct way to write the underlined part of sentence 16.

   <u>The recycling box go</u> next to the garbage.

   f. The recycling box goes
   g. The recycling boxes goes
   h. The recycling box going
   j. No change is needed.

9. Choose the sentence that does **not** belong in the paragraph that begins with sentence 5.

   a. sentence 5
   b. sentence 12
   c. sentence 14
   d. sentence 9

10. Choose the correct way to write the underlined part of sentence 13.

   The cans and jars <u>went</u> in the same big box.

   f. were
   g. have
   h. go
   j. No change is needed.

11

Andrey is in the third grade. His class is learning about classical music. His teacher asked each student to write about a famous composer. Andrey chose Mozart. He went to the library and took notes. Now he needs your help editing and revising his rough draft.

Here is Andrey's rough draft. Read it and then answer questions 1–10.

(1) wolfgang amadeus Mozart was born in 1756. (2) He was Austrian. (3) His father was musician, too. (4) Mozart started learning the harpsichord when he was four. (5) He started writeing music when he was five! (6) When he was six, he plays for the queen.

(7) Mozart wrote all types of music. (8) He wrote the kind that people sing in church. (9) He also wrote operas and symphonies. (10) He wrote a lot of music for string quartets. (11) A string quartet has two violins a viola and a cello.

(12) Composers didn't make good money back then. (13) Mozart was very poor when he died. (14) He lived since thirty-five years. (15) Mozart had accomplished a lot by the time he died when he was thirty-five.

1. Choose the correct way to write the underlined part of sentence 1.

   wolfgang amadeus Mozart was born in 1756.

   a. Wolfgang amadeus Mozart
   b. Wolfgang Amadeus Mozart
   c. wolfgang amadeus Mozart
   d. No change is needed.

2. Choose the topic sentence for the paragraph that begins with sentence 7.

   f. Mozart wrote all types of music.
   g. He wrote the kind that people sing in church.
   h. He also wrote operas and symphonies.
   j. He wrote a lot of music for string quartets.

3. Choose the correct way to write the underlined part of sentence 3.

His father <u>was musician, too.</u>

a. was a musician, too.
b. was an musician, too.
c. was am musician, too.
d. No change is needed.

4. Choose the sentence that **best** fits right after sentence 13.

f. The 1700s were a long time ago.
g. Austria is a European country that is close to Germany.
h. He would have liked to live in the 21st century.
j. If he lived in this day and age, he may have been a rich man.

5. Choose the correct way to write the underlined part of sentence 6.

When he was six, <u>he plays for the queen.</u>

a. he play for the queen.
b. he is playing for the queen.
c. he played for the queen.
d. No change is needed.

6. Which one of these is **not** a complete sentence?

    f. He wrote the kind that people sing in church.
    g. He was Austrian.
    h. He also wrote opera and symphonies.
    j. A lot of music for string quartets.

7. Choose the correct way to write the underlined part of sentence 11.

    A string quartet has <u>two violins a viola and a cello.</u>

    a. two violins, a viola, and a cello.
    b. two violins, a viola, and, a cello.
    c. two, violins a, viola and a, cello.
    d. No change is needed.

8. Choose the correct way to write sentence 14.

    He lived since only thirty-five years.

    f. He lived until only thirty-five years.
    g. He lived for only thirty-five years.
    h. He lived since only he was thirty-five years.
    j. No change is needed.

9. Choose the **best** way to combine the ideas in sentences 14 and 15 into one sentence.

> **He lived since thirty-five years. Mozart had accomplished a lot by the time he died when he was thirty-five.**

a. Mozart accomplished a lot by thirty-five.
b. Mozart accomplished a lot by the time he died in 1935.
c. Mozart died at only thirty-five by accomplishing a lot.
d. Although he died when he was only thirty-five, Mozart accomplished a lot.

10. Choose the correct way to write the underlined part of sentence 5.

> **He started <u>writeing</u> music when he was five!**

f. writting
g. riting
h. writing
j. No change is needed.

Emily is in the third grade. Her class is learning about the oceans of the world. Her teacher asked each student to choose one ocean or sea and write about it. Emily chose the Arctic Ocean. Her rough draft is done, but now she needs your help editing and revising it.

Here is Emily's rough draft. Read it and then answer questions 1–10.

---

(1) The Arctic Ocean is <u>the smallest Ocean in the world.</u> (2) It is above the Arctic Circle. (3) It is extremely cold. (4) In the winter, it is almost all covered with ice. (5) <u>Glacier's</u> are huge pieces of ice. (6) <u>Glacier float</u> in the water. (7) Some of them are so big that they are like <u>ilands.</u> (8) Scientists build stations on them. (9) At these stations, they can do all sorts of experiments.

(10) A few kinds of animals live in the Arctic Ocean. (11) There are fish and seals. (12) There are polar bears, too. (13) There are whales, too. (14) The whales eat plankton. (15) Plankton are tiny animals or plants <u>that floats</u> in the sea. (16) There aren't very many plants in the <u>Arctic Ocean There</u> is not enough sunlight and it is too cold. (17) It is very cold in Antarctica, too.

---

1. Choose the correct way to write the underlined part of sentence 1.

   The Arctic Ocean is <u>the smallest Ocean in the world.</u>

   a. the smallest ocean in the world.
   b. the smallest ocean in the World.
   c. the smallest Ocean in the World.
   d. No change is needed.

2. Choose the topic sentence for the paragraph that begins with sentence 10.

   f. A few kinds of animals live in the Arctic Ocean.
   g. There are fish and seals.
   h. The whales eat plankton.
   j. It is very cold in Antarctica, too.

3. Choose the correct way to write the underlined part of sentence 5.

<u>Glacier's</u> are huge pieces of ice.

a. Glaciers'
b. glaciers
c. Glaciers
d. No change is needed.

4. Choose the sentence that does **not** belong in the paragraph that begins with sentence 10.

f. sentence 10
g. sentence 12
h. sentence 14
j. sentence 17

5. Choose the correct way to write the underlined part of sentence 6.

<u>Glacier float</u> in the water.

a. Glaciers float
b. Glacier floats
c. Glacier it floats
d. No change is needed.

17

6. Choose the **best** way to combine the ideas in sentences 11, 12, and 13 into one sentence.

> **There are fish and seals. There are polar bears, too. There are whales, too.**

   f. There are fish, seals, polar bears, and whales.
   g. Fish, seals, polar, bears and whales.
   h. Fish, seals, and whales all live in the ocean.
   j. Fish, seals, polar, bears and whales are all animals.

7. Choose the correct way to write the underlined part of sentence 15.

> **Plankton are tiny animals and plants <u>that floats</u> in the sea.**

   a. that float
   b. that floating
   c. that floated
   d. No change is needed.

8. Choose the correct way to write the underlined part of sentence 16.

> **There aren't very many plants in the <u>Arctic Ocean There</u> is not enough sunlight and it is too cold.**

   f. Arctic Ocean? There
   g. Arctic Ocean, There
   h. Arctic Ocean. There
   j. No change is needed.

9. Choose the correct way to write the underlined part of sentence 7.

   Some of them are so big that they are like <u>ilands.</u>

   a. i-lands.
   b. islands.
   c. ilends.
   d. No change is needed.

10. Choose the **best** way to combine the ideas in sentences 8 and 9 into one sentence.

    Scientists build stations on them. At these stations, they can do all sorts of experiments.

    f. Scientists build stations on them and do all sorts of experiments.
    g. Scientists build experiments on stations.
    h. Scientists build stations on them by doing all sorts of experiments.
    j. Scientists build stations on the experiments.

Brian is in the third grade. His class is learning how to write invitations. His teacher asked each student to write an invitation to a classmate. Brian decided to invite his classmate to go bowling. First he wrote down some ideas that he wanted to include in the invitation. Then he wrote his rough draft. Now he needs help editing and revising it.

Here is Brian's rough draft. Read it and then answer questions 1–10.

---

(1) dear Jared,

(2) Do you know how to bowl? (3) I do I started bowling last year. (4) It's probaly my favorite sport now. (5) I joined a youth team at Penny Lanes. (6) I bowl for my team every week, and sometimes I practicing on the weekend.

(7) You don't need anything special to start bowling. (8) All you need is patience. (9) At first, I threw most of the balls into the gutter. (10) Now, I usually get at least one strike or spare.

(11) Would you like to try bowling! (12) If you go with me on Saturday, my coach will be there. (13) He can teach you, too. (14) There are vending machines.

(15) Bowling is good exercise and it's a lot of fun. (16) It's a blast! (17) I hope you will try it. (18) Please let me know if you are interested. (19) Only if interested.

(20) your friend,

(21) Brian

---

1. Choose the correct way to write line 1, the opening of the letter.

    dear Jared,

    a. dear jared,
    b. Dear Jared,
    c. Deer Jared,
    d. No change is needed.

2. Read sentence 3. It is poorly written.

I do I started bowling last year.

Choose the **best** way to rewrite this sentence.

    f. I do for that I started bowling last year.
    g. I do and I started bowling last year.
    h. I do! I started bowling last year.
    j. I do when I started bowling last year.

3. Choose the correct way to write the underlined part of sentence 4.

It's <u>probaly</u> my favorite sport now.

    a. probably
    b. probly
    c. probally
    d. No change is needed.

4. Choose the sentence that does **not** belong in the paragraph that begins with sentence 11.

    f. sentence 11
    g. sentence 12
    h. sentence 13
    j. sentence 14

5. Choose the correct way to write the underlined part of sentence 6.

   I bowl for my team every week, and sometimes <u>I practicing</u> on the weekend.

   a. I practiced
   b. I practice
   c. I was practicing
   d. No change is needed.

6. Which one of these is **not** a complete sentence?

   f. He can teach you, too.
   g. All you need is patience.
   h. Please let me know if you are interested.
   j. Only if interested.

7. Choose the correct way to write the underlined part of sentence 11.

   Would you like <u>to try bowling!</u>

   a. to try bowling?
   b. to try bowling.
   c. to try bowling,
   d. No change is needed.

8. Choose the **best** way to combine the ideas in sentences 15 and 16 into one sentence.

Bowling is good exercise and it's alot of fun. It's a blast!

f. Bowling is good exercise, and it's a blast!
g. Blasting is a bowl of fun exercise.
h. Bowling is a blast of exercise.
j. The blast about bowling is that it's good exercise.

9. Choose the correct way to write line 20, the closing of the letter.

your friend,

a. Your Friend,
b. You friend,
c. Your friend,
d. No change is needed.

10. Brian wants to add this sentence to the paragraph that begins with sentence 2, the paragraph that begins with sentence 7, or the paragraph that begins with sentence 15.

That's because it's not as easy as it looks!

Where would the sentence **best** fit?

f. right after sentence 4
g. right after sentence 7
h. right after sentence 8
j. right after sentence 19

Moojig's third-grade class is studying Native Americans. His teacher asked each student to imagine life as a child in the Wampanoag tribe. Each student wrote a journal entry describing his or her day as a Wampanoag child. Moojig brainstormed his ideas and made a list. Next, he thought about how to put his ideas together. Then, he wrote his rough draft. He needs your help editing and revising it.

Here is Moojig's rough draft. Read it and then answer questions 1–11.

(1) I am a Wampanoag boy. (2) Let me tell you what I did today.

(3) I woke up this morning when the sun rose. (4) I brushed my teeth with mint leaves. (5) I used pine bristles for a toothbrush. (6) <u>There was beans and squash</u> for breakfast. (7) Last year, we had a long, hard winter.

(8) My first job was corn sitting. (9) <u>I am sitting in the tower</u> and shooed the birds away from the corn. (10) My sisters and mother went out to gather wood for the cooking fire. (11) I went with my father to catch fish. (12) I caught a trout today, and <u>we had for dinner.</u> (13) I set a turkey trap, too, but it <u>didnt</u> catch anything.

(14) I think my father is <u>the bestest hunter</u> in the tribe. (15) My older brother knows how to use a bow and arrow. (16) I can't wait to start hunting with a bow and arrow.

(17) It's getting late so it's time for bed. (18) I am going <u>back home.</u> (19) I had a good today. (20) It was fun.

1. Choose the correct way to write the underlined part of sentence 6.

    <u>There was beans and squash</u> for breakfast.

    a. They was beans and squash
    b. There were beans and squash
    c. There is beans and squash
    d. No change is needed.

24

2. Choose the sentence that does **not** belong in the paragraph that begins with sentence 3.

   f. sentence 5
   g. sentence 4
   h. sentence 7
   j. sentence 3

3. Choose the correct way to write the underlined part of sentence 9.

   <u>I am sitting in the tower</u> and shooed the birds away from the corn.

   a. I will sit in the tower
   b. I sit in the tower
   c. I sat in the tower
   d. No change is needed.

4. Read sentence 19. It is poorly written.

   I had a good today.

   Choose the **best** way to rewrite this sentence.

   f. It was a good one.
   g. I had a good day today.
   h. Today rocked.
   j. I was good today.

25

5. Choose the correct way to write the underlined part of sentence 12.

I caught a trout today, and <u>we had for dinner.</u>

a. we had it for dinner.
b. we had him for dinner.
c. we had them for dinner.
d. No change is needed.

6. Choose the best way to combine the ideas in sentences 15 and 16 into one sentence.

My older brother knows how to use a bow and arrow. I can't wait to start hunting with a bow and arrow.

f. I can't wait to start hunting with one, too.
g. I can't wait to start hunting with a bow and arrow like my older brother.
h. I can't wait to start hunting with my older brother.
j. I can't wait!

7. Choose the correct way to write the underlined part of sentence 13.

I set a turkey trap, too, but it <u>didnt</u> catch anything.

a. didin't
b. didn't
c. didn't
d. No change is needed.

26

8. Moojig wants to add this sentence to the paragraph that begins with sentence 17.

I can't wait for tomorrow.

Where would this sentence **best** fit?

f. right after sentence 17
g. right after sentence 20
h. right after sentence 18
j. right after sentence 19

9. Choose the correct way to write the underlined part of sentence 14.

I think my father is <u>the bestest hunter</u> in the tribe.

a. a better hunter
b. the better hunter
c. the best hunter
d. No change is needed.

10. Moojig wants to change sentence 17 so that it is more specific.

<u>It's getting late</u> so it's time for bed.

Choose the **best** way to rewrite the underlined part of this sentence.

f. It's late
g. The sun is setting now and I'm feeling sleepy
h. It's getting dark now
j. The sun is going down

11. Choose the correct way to write the underlined part of sentence 18.

I am going <u>back home.</u>

   a. back home!
   b. back home,
   c. back home?
   d. No change is needed.

Haneet is in the third grade. Her teacher asked each student to write a letter to a friend. Haneet decided to write about her trip to the steam train museum. She wrote her rough draft, but now she need help editing and revising it.

Here is Haneet's rough draft. Read it and then answer questions 1–10.

(1) Dear anna,

    (2) I had a lot of fun last weekend. (3) I went to the steam train museum. (4) It was <u>funner than</u> the dinosaur park! (5) I was in the second grade last year.

    (6) We got to ride a real steam train! (7) It was so <u>exiting!</u> (8) The train had coal for fuel. (9) First, the engineer checked the engine. (10) Then he shouted, "All aboard!" (11) I loved the sound of the whistle and the hissing steam. (12) The train was loud-sounding.

    (13) The train took us <u>through the woods.</u> (14) It was beautiful. (15) We went past streams and ponds, and we saw many birds. (16) I saw a woodpecker! (17) We <u>will go</u> all the way to the station in the next town. (18) A few passengers got on the riverboat ride there.

    (19) You should ride a steam train sometime. (20) It's a day great to spend. (21) <u>Im</u> sure you will like it, too!

                              (22) Your friend,

                              (23) Haneet

1. Choose the correct way to write line 1, the opening of the letter.

    Dear anna,

    a. Dear Anna,
    b. Dear anna.
    c. Deer anna
    d. No change is needed.

2. Choose the topic sentence for the paragraph that begins with sentence 6.

    f. I loved the sound of the whistle and the hissing steam.
    g. We got to ride a real steam train!
    h. The train had coal for fuel.
    j. Then he shouted, "All aboard!"

3. Choose the correct way to write the underlined part of sentence 4.

It was <u>funner than</u> the dinosaur park!

    a. more funner than
    b. funnest than
    c. more fun than
    d. No change is needed.

4. Choose the correct way to write the underlined part of sentence 7.

It was so <u>exiting!</u>

    f. exitting.
    g. exciting!
    h. exciteing!
    j. No change is needed.

5. Choose the sentence that does **not** belong in the paragraph that begins with sentence 2.

    a. sentence 4
    b. sentence 3
    c. sentence 5
    d. sentence 2

6. Choose the correct way to write the underlined part of sentence 13.

   The train took us <u>through the woods.</u>

   f. threw the woods.
   g. though the woods.
   h. thru the woods.
   j. No change is needed.

7. Haneet wants to change sentence 12 so that it is more specific.

   The train was loud-sounding.

   Choose the **best** way to rewrite the sentence.

   a. The wheels on the track made a loud "clickety-clack" sound.
   b. The train made a neat sound.
   c. The train was loud.
   d. The wheels made a loud and cool clacking sound.

8. Choose the correct way to write the underlined part of sentence 21.

   <u>Im</u> sure you will like it, too!

   f. i'm
   g. I'm
   h. Im'
   j. No change is needed.

9. Read sentence 20. It is poorly written.

   It's a day great to spend.

   Choose the **best** way to rewrite this sentence.

   a. It's a great way to spend a day.
   b. Great is the day to spend.
   c. It's a day of spending.
   d. Spending a day is great.

10. Choose the correct way to write the underlined part of sentence 17.

    We <u>will go</u> all the way to the station in the next town.

    f. went
    g. were going
    h. are going
    j. No change is needed.

32

Luz is in the third grade. Her class is learning about mammals. Her teacher asked each student to choose one type of mammal and to write a report about it. Luz chose to write about bats. She wrote her rough draft, but now she needs your help editing and revising it.

Here is Luz's rough draft. Read it and then answer questions 1–10.

(1) Why are people so scared of <u>bats.</u> (2) Bats do not hurt people. (3) They are good and interesting animals.

(4) Bats are mammals. (5) That means that bat babies drink their mothers' milk. (6) Some bats eat fruit, and <u>some eat fish, Vampire bats drink blood</u> from animals. (7) Don't worry, though. (8) These particular bats live in <u>Central and South america.</u> (9) There are giant pythons down there, too!

(10) People think that bats can't see. (11) They can! (12) <u>They can use sound,</u> too. (13) They make sounds and the sounds bounce off things. (14) <u>The bats listens</u> to the echo. (15) Then they know where they are.

(16) Bats are good for us. (17) They eat bugs. (18) They also help plants to spread their seeds. (19) Do not be afraid of bats.

(20) In the United States, brown bats go to sleep all winter. (21) You can find them in dark caves in the winter. (22) If you're brave enough to venture into one!

1. Choose the correct way to write the underlined part of sentence 1.

   Why are people so scared of <u>bats.</u>

   a. bats!
   b. bats,
   c. bats?
   d. No change is needed.

2. Choose the topic sentence of this composition.

    f. Bats do no hurt people.
    g. They are good and interesting animals.
    h. They are mammals.
    j. they also help plants to spread their seeds.

3. Choose the correct way to write the underlined part of sentence 8.

These particular bats live in <u>Central and South america.</u>

    a. Central and south America.
    b. central and South America.
    c. Central and South America.
    d. No change is needed.

4. Which one of these is **not** a complete sentence?

    f. If you're brave enough to venture into one!
    g. They eat bugs.
    h. They can!
    j. Bats are good for people.

5. Choose the correct way to write the underlined part of sentence 12.

<u>They can use sound,</u> too.

    a. They used sound,
    b. They were able to use sound,
    c. They were using sound,
    d. No change is needed.

6. Choose the sentence that does **not** belong in the paragraph that begins with sentence 4.

    f. sentence 7
    g. sentence 5
    h. sentence 9
    j. sentence 4

7. Choose the correct way to write the underlined part of sentence 6.

Some bats eat fruit, and <u>some eat fish, Vampire bats drink blood</u> from animals.

    a. some eat fish. Vampire bats drink blood
    b. some eat fish? Vampire bats drink blood
    c. some eat fish Vampire bats drink blood
    d. No change is needed.

8. Choose the **best** way to combine the ideas in sentences 20 and 21 into one sentence.

In the United States, brown bats go to sleep all winter. You can find them in dark caves in the winter.

    f. In the United States, brown bats sleep in caves.
    g. In the United States, you can find brown bats sleeping in caves through all of winter
    h. In the United States winter, brown bats are in caves sleeping.
    j. In the United States, caves are where you find sleeping bats.

9. Choose the correct way to write the underlined part of sentence 14.

   <u>The bats listens</u> to the echo.

   a. The bats listen
   b. The bats listening
   c. The bat listen
   d. No change is needed.

10. Luz wants to add this sentence to the paragraph that begins with sentence 16.

    Like other animals, they are probably more afraid of us than we are of them.

    Where would the sentence **best** fit?

    f. right after sentence 16
    g. right after sentence 17
    h. right after sentence 19
    j. right after sentence 18

Jeff's third-grade class is learning about Egypt. His teacher asked each student to write a short report. Jeff has written his rough draft, and now he needs your help editing and revising it.

Here is Jeff's rough draft. Read it and then answer questions 1–11.

(1) An important part of life in <u>ancient</u> Egypt was mummification. (2) Why did the Egyptians make <u>mummies</u> (3) They believed that they should save the bodies <u>for there next lives.</u> (4) The Egyptians took good care of the bodies of their dead. (5) They wrapped them up in linen. (6) Some of the mummies have lasted until today. (7) Some people in Egypt even turned pets into mummies! (8) There are mummies of cats and monkeys. (9) I always wanted a monkey.

(10) Egyptians put a lot of things into the tombs with the mummies they thought they would be able to use them in the next life. (11) They put <u>food clothes jewelry and other things</u> into the tombs. (12) Rich people even had statues of servants. (13) <u>They think</u> that the statues would come to life someday and do work for them.

(14) There are nice pictures on the wall of tombs. (15) In these pictures, everybody looks young and beautiful. (16) <u>They look more nice</u> than they did in real life. (17) That's because the people thought pictures could come to life, too!

1. Choose the correct way to write the underlined part of sentence 2.

   Why did the Egyptians make <u>mummies</u>

   a. mummies!
   b. mummies.
   c. mummies?
   d. No change is needed.

2. Choose the sentence that does **not** belong in the paragraph that begins with sentence 1.

   f. sentence 6
   g. sentence 9
   h. sentence 7
   j. sentence 8

3. Choose the correct way to write the underlined part of sentence 3.

   They believed that they should save the bodies <u>for there next lives.</u>

   a. for their next lives.
   b. for they're next lives?
   c. for they are next lives.
   d. No change is needed.

4. Jeff wants to add this sentence to the paragraph that begins with sentence 14.

   They are paintings, not photos, because there were no cameras back then.

   Where would the sentence **best** fit?

   f. right after sentence 16
   g. right after sentence 17
   h. right after sentence 14
   j. right after sentence 15

38

5. Choose the correct way to write the underlined part of sentence 11.

   They put <u>food clothes jewelry and other things</u> into the tombs.

   a. food. Also clothes, jewelry, and other things
   b. food, clothes, jewelry, and other things
   c. food, and clothes and jewelry and other things
   d. No change is needed.

6. Read sentence 10. It is poorly written.

   Egyptians put a lot of things into the tombs with the mummies they thought they would be able to use them in the next life.

   Choose the **best** way to rewrite this sentence.

   f. Egyptians put a lot of things into the tombs with the mummies that which they thought they would be able to use them in the next life.
   g. Egyptians put a lot of things into the tombs. With the mummies they thought they would be able to use them in the next life.
   h. Egyptians put a lot of things into the tombs with the mummies, they thought. They would be able to use them in the next life.
   j. Egyptians put a lot of things into the tombs with the mummies. They thought they would be able to use them in the next life.

7. Choose the correct way to write the underlined part of sentence 13.

   <u>They think</u> that the statues would come to life someday and do work for them.

   a. They thought
   b. They are thinking
   c. They will think
   d. No change is needed.

8. Choose the topic sentence of this report.

    f. Egyptians put a lot of things into the tombs with the mummies they thought they would be able to use them in the next life.

    g. An important part of life in ancient Egypt was mummification.

    h. The Egyptians took good care of the bodies of their dead.

    j. They believed that they should save the bodies for their next lives.

9. Choose the correct way to write the underlined part of sentence 16.

    <u>They look more nice</u> than they did in real life.

    a. They look more nice

    b. They look beautifuller

    c. They look better

    d. No change is needed.

10. Jeff wants to add this sentence to the paragraph that begins with sentence 14.

    Can you imagine a picture coming to life?

    Where would the sentence **best** fit?

    f. right after sentence 17

    g. right after sentence 14

    h. right after sentence 15

    j. right after sentence 16

[Spelling]

11. Choose the correct way to write the underlined part of sentence 1.

    An important part of life in <u>ancient</u> Egypt was mummification.

    a. anchent
    b. anchint
    c. anchient
    d. No change is needed.

Jada is in the third grade. Her class recently visited the children's museum. Her teacher asked each student to write a letter to a friend describing his or her day. Jada used a graphic organizer to put her ideas in order. Then she wrote her rough draft, and she needs your help editing and revising it.

Here is Jada's rough draft. Read it and then answer questions 1–11.

---

(1) Dear Kayla,

(2) I had a great time last week it was so fun. (3) <u>My class went</u> to the children's museum. (4) You should go, to.

(5) We rode a school bus for an hour <u>to get their.</u> (6) The first thing was a tour. (7) The tour of the whole museum was the very first thing we did. (8) We spent time in each section. (9) My favorite part was the train. (10) Driving the train was that which I liked the most. (11) <u>There were a camera</u> on the front of the engine. (12) I <u>cood</u> see everything on the screen!

(13) We had a rainforest workshop. (14) It was fun! (15) We learned about animal habitats. (16) I didn't know ants and trees help each other. (17) Azteca ants live on the acacia tree. (18) When something attacks the tree, the ants fight back!

(19) The museum fed us lunch. (20) Maybe you can go there sometime. (21) It's so much fun! (22) Another good thing to do is to go to the police museum.

(23) Your friend

(24) Jada

---

1. Choose the correct way to write the underlined part of sentence 3.

   <u>My class went</u> to the children's museum.

   a. My class goes
   b. My class go
   c. My class going
   d. No change is needed.

42

2. Read sentence 2. It is poorly written.

   I had a great time last week it was so fun.

   Choose the **best** way to rewrite this sentence.

   f. I had a great time last week, it was so fun.
   g. I had a great time last week and it was so much fun.
   h. I had a great time last week so it was so much fun.
   j. I had a great time last week. It was so much fun.

3. Choose the correct way to write sentence 4.

   You should go, to.

   a. You should go, too.
   b. You should go, two.
   c. You should go to.
   d. No change is needed.

4. Choose the **best** way to combine the ideas in sentences 6 and 7 into one sentence.

   The first thing was a tour. The tour of the whole museum was the very first thing we did.

   f. The first thing that we did was a tour of the whole museum.
   g. That we did first was a tour of the whole museum.
   h. The whole museum was the first tour.
   j. The whole museum had a tour at first.

43

5. Choose the correct way to write the underlined part of sentence 5.

   We rode a school bus for an hour <u>to get their.</u>

   a. to get they're.
   b. to get there.
   c. to get they are.
   d. No change is needed.

6. Jada wants to change sentence 19 so that it is more specific.

   The museum fed us lunch.

   Choose the **best** way to rewrite the sentence.

   f. The museum fed us a hot and delicious lunch.
   g. The museum gave us a good lunch.
   h. The museum served us a hot and delicious lunch of turkey, mashed potatoes, and cornbread.
   j. For lunch, we ate at the museum.

7. Choose the correct way to write the underlined part of sentence 11.

   <u>There were a camera</u> on the front of the engine.

   a. There are a camera
   b. There was a camera
   c. There was cameras
   d. No change is needed.

8. Choose the sentence that does **not** belong in the paragraph that begins with sentence 19.

   f. sentence 19
   g. sentence 20
   h. sentence 21
   j. sentence 22

9. Choose the correct way to write the underlined part of sentence 12.

   I <u>cood</u> see everything on the screen!

   a. cold
   b. coud
   c. could
   d. No change is needed.

10. Read sentence 10. It is poorly written.

    Driving the train was that which I liked the most.

    Choose the **best** way to rewrite this sentence.

    f. I liked driving the train the best.
    g. The train was the best.
    h. Driving the train was that which was the best part to me.
    j. I liked that I could drive the train best.

45

11. Choose the correct way to write line 23, the closing of the letter.

Your friend

a. Your friend,
b. Yours, friend
c. Your Friend
d. No change is needed.

Nicole is in the third grade. Her class is studying health. Her teacher asked each student to write about how to stay healthy during flu and cold season. Nicole put her notes into a graphic organizer. Then she wrote a rough draft. Now she needs help editing and revising it.

Here is Nicole's rough draft. Read it and then answer questions 1–10.

(1) It's important to stay healthy <u>through</u> cold and flu season. (2) You don't want to catch a cold. (3) Here is how you can avoid getting sick.

(4) The first thing you should do is to eat right.   (5) Make sure you eat <u>enuff</u> fresh fruits and vegetables. (6) If you don't, your immune system will be weak. (7) The immune system is the <u>bodys's</u> defense against germs. (8) <u>Oranges and orange juice and green vegetables</u> make it strong.

(9) Another thing you can do is to wash your hands. (10) Wash your hands thoroughly. (11) You should sing the "Happy Birthday" song while you wash your hands.   (12) The length of that song is that's how long which it will take.

(13) When you are sick, you should think about the people around you. (14) They don't want your germs! (15) If you sneeze or cough into your hands, <u>wash it right away.</u>

(16) Now you know the best ways to avoid getting sick. (17) Drink you're orange juice and wash you're hands!

1. Choose the correct way to write the underlined part of sentence 1.

   It's important to stay healthy <u>through</u> cold and flu season.

   a. thru
   b. threw
   c. thorough
   d. No change is needed.

2. Choose the topic sentence for the paragraph that begins with sentence 9.

    f. Wash your hands thoroughly.

    g. You should sing the "Happy Birthday" song while you wash your hands.

    h. The length of that song is that's how long which it will take.

    j. Another thing you can do is to wash your hands.

3. Choose the correct way to write the underlined part of sentence 5.

    Make sure you eat <u>enuff</u> fresh fruits and vegetables.

    a. enuf

    b. enough

    c. enugh

    d. No change is needed.

4. Choose the sentence that **best** fits right after sentence 15.

    f. Whole grains and nuts are good, too.

    g. You could also sing "Yankee Doodle."

    h. Don't forget to use hot water and lots of soap.

    j. Good food is packed with vitamins and minerals.

5. Choose the correct way to write the underlined part of sentence 7.

    The immune system is the <u>bodys's</u> defense against germs.

    a. body's

    b. bodies

    c. bodies'

    d. No change is needed.

6. Nicole wants to add these sentences to the paragraph that begins with sentence 13.

   One last important thing that you need to do is to get lots of sleep. Getting plenty of sleep helps us to fight off germs and to stay healthy.

   Where would the sentences **best** fit?

   f. right before sentence 13
   g. right after sentence 13
   h. right after sentence 15
   j. right after sentence 14

7. Choose the correct way to write the underlined part of sentence 8.

   <u>**Oranges and orange juice and green vegetables**</u> **make it strong.**

   a. Oranges—orange juice—and green vegetables
   b. Oranges and orange juice, green vegetables
   c. Oranges, orange juice, and green vegetables
   d. No change is needed.

8. Read sentence 12. It is poorly written.

   The length of that song is that's how long which it will take.

   Choose the **best** way to rewrite this sentence.

   f. You should wash your hands for the length of it.
   g. The washing should take the song.
   h. You should wash your hands for about as long as it takes to sing that song.
   j. The length of that song is how long which it will take.

9. Choose the correct way to write the underlined part of sentence 15.

   If you sneeze or cough into your hands, <u>wash it right away.</u>

   a. wash 'em right away.
   b. wash them right away.
   c. wash this right away.
   d. No change is needed.

10. Choose the correct way to write sentence 17.

    Drink you're orange juice and wash you're hands!

    f. Drink your orange juice and wash your hands!
    g. Drink you'r orange juice and wash you'r hands!
    h. Drink yore orange juice and wash yore hands!
    j. No change is needed.

Beth's third-grade class is studying inventions. Her teacher asked each student to write a report about one of Eli Whitney's inventions. Beth chose the cotton gin. She took notes at the school library, and then she wrote a rough draft. Now she needs help editing and revising it.

Here is Beth's rough draft. Read it and then answer questions 1–11.

(1) Eli Whitney invented <u>the cotton gin?</u> (2) Whitney was widely known as a very talented man. (3) His friends said, "He can build anything!" (4) Believe it or not, I have a friend who lives on Eli Whitney Avenue.

(5) Eli Whitney <u>came from massachusetts.</u> (6) He went to Yale, and then he moved south in 1793. (7) He moved to Georgia at this time. (8) He wanted to teach.

(9) In Georgia, Eli <u>discuvered</u> that cotton farmers had a problem. (10) <u>They had too separate</u> the cotton from its sticky green seeds. (11) Difficult was the work and a long time it took. (12) Eli watched. (13) The way cotten was cleaned.

(14) He built a machine out of hooks, wires and spinning brushes. (15) It could clean cotton very quickly. (16) Eli made more machines. (17) Farmers <u>brung</u> their cotton to the gins to get cleaned.

(18) However, some of the farmers made <u>their</u> own cotton gins. (19) This made Eli angry because he had a patent. (20) A patent law was supposed to stop other people from copying his invention, but it didn't work. (21) He didn't make any money on his cotton gin.

1. Choose the correct way to write the underlined part of sentence 1.

   Eli Whitney invented <u>the cotton gin?</u>

   a. the cotton gin!
   b. the cotton gin.
   c. the cotton gin,
   d. No change is needed.

2. Choose the sentence that does **not** belong in the paragraph that begins with sentence 1.

   f. sentence1
   g. sentence 2
   h. sentence 3
   j. sentence 4

3. Choose the correct way to write the underlined part of sentence 5.

   Eli Whitney <u>came from massachusetts.</u>

   a. is from massachusetts.
   b. from massachusetts.
   c. came from Massachusetts.
   d. No change is needed.

4. Choose the **best** way to combine the ideas in sentences 12 and 13 into one sentence.

   Eli watched. The way the cotton was cleaned.

   f. Eli watched the way the cotton was cleaned.
   g. Eli watched! the way the cotton was cleaned.
   h. Eli cleaned the cotton.
   j. The way the cotton was cleaned was what Eli watched.

5. Choose the correct way to write the underlined part of sentence 9.

   In Georgia, Eli <u>discuvered</u> that cotton farmers had a problem.

   a. discovered
   b. descovered
   c. discoveried
   d. No change is needed.

6. Choose the **best** way to combine the ideas in sentences 6 and 7 into one sentence.

He went to Yale, and then he moved south in 1793. He moved to Georgia at this time.

   f. He went to Yale, and then he moved south in 1793, to Georgia.
   g. He went to Yale, and then in 1793, at this time, he moved south to Georgia.
   h. He moved south to Georgia at the time after he went to Yale.
   j. He went to Yale, and then he moved south to Georgia in 1793.

7. Choose the correct way to write the underlined part of sentence 10.

<u>They had too separate</u> the cotton from its sticky green seeds.

   a. They had toe separate
   b. They had to separate
   c. They had two separate
   d. No change is needed.

8. Read sentence 11. It is poorly written.

Difficult was the work and a long time it took.

Choose the **best** way to rewrite this sentence.

   f. The work was long time and difficult.
   g. The work took long and difficult time.
   h. The work was difficult and took a long time.
   j. The work was difficult and long was the time it took.

53

9. Choose the correct way to write the underlined part of sentence 17.

   Farmers <u>brung</u> their cotton to the gins to get cleaned.

   a. brang
   b. brought
   c. bringed
   d. No change is needed.

10. Beth wants to add this sentence to the paragraph that begins with sentence 1.

    This invention is one of the greatest in America's history.

    Where would the sentence **best** fit?

    f. right after sentence 1
    g. right after sentence 2
    h. right after sentence 3
    j. right after sentence 4

11. Choose the correct way to write the underlined part of sentence 18.

    However, some of the farmers made <u>their</u> own cotton gins.

    a. they're
    b. there
    c. theirs
    d. No change is needed.

Gina's third-grade class is learning about transportation. Her teacher asked her to pretend to be a car, bus, plane, train, or ship and write a short story. Gina chose to be an airplane. She wrote her rough draft, and now she needs your help editing and revising it.

Here is Gina's rough draft. Read it and then answer questions 1–11.

(1) I am a Boeing 777 jet. (2) I am getting ready for my big flight to <u>Orlando Florida.</u> (3) I have two engines. (4) Don't worry, though? (5) If one engine fails, I can still fly for two hours. (6) An airport can still be gotten to by the pilot with enough time. (7) Therefore, nothing to worry about.

(8) My baggage compartment has a lot of stuff in it. (9) Many people are traveling for <u>thanksgiving.</u> (10) The air traffic controllers are checking the <u>flite</u> plan. (11) The captain and flight officer are talking. (12) They are talking in the cockpit. (13) They have to decide who will be the flying pilot and who will be the non-flying pilot. (14) Each pilot has different jobs to do.

(15) It's raining hard. (16) It's <u>more bad than</u> this morning. (17) They told me that I had to sit in this runway for an hour. (18) I'm so bored!

(19) The captain just got permission to take off! (20) Now I am climbing to five thousand feet. (21) Pretty soon, I'll be thirty-seven thousand feet over the Atlantic Ocean. (22) Florida, here we come!

1. Choose the correct way to write the underlined part of sentence 2.

   I am getting ready for my big flight to <u>Orlando Florida.</u>

   a. orlando, florida.
   b. Orlando, Florida.
   c. Orlando Florida,
   d. No change is needed.

55

2. Read sentence 6. It is poorly written.

    An airport can still be gotten to by the pilot with enough time.

    Choose the **best** way to rewrite this sentence.

    f. The pilot could still get me to an airport.
    g. That's enough time for an airport.
    h. That's enough time for a pilot to get me to an airport.
    j. An airport can still be gotten to by the pilot with enough of the time.

3. Choose the correct way to write sentence 4.

    Don't worry, though?

    a. Don't worry, though.
    b. Don't worry, though,
    c. Don't worry, though!
    d. No change is needed.

4. Gina wants to change sentence 8 so that it is more specific.

    My baggage compartment <u>has a lot of stuff in it.</u>

    Choose the **best** way to rewrite the underlined part of this sentence.

    f. has a lot of suitcases.
    g. is filled with suitcases, boxes, and even crates of animals.
    h. has tons of baggage like suitcases and boxes.
    j. is full.

5. Choose the correct way to write the underlined part of sentence 9.

    Many people are traveling for <u>thanksgiving.</u>

    a. thanksgiving.
    b. thanks Giving.
    c. Thanksgiving.
    d. No change is needed.

6. Choose the **best** way to combine the ideas in sentence 11 and 12 into one sentence.

    The captain and flight officer are talking. They are talking in the cockpit.

    f. The captain and flight officer are talking and they are doing this in the cockpit.
    g. The captain and flight officer are talking in the cockpit.
    h. The captain and flight officer are talking, in the cockpit.
    j. The captain and flight officer in the cockpit are talking.

7. Choose the correct way to write the underlined part of sentence 16.

    It's <u>more bad than</u> this morning.

    a. worse than
    b. badder than
    c. worst than
    d. No change is needed.

8. Read sentence 7. It is poorly written.

   Therefore, nothing to worry about.

   Choose the **best** way to rewrite the sentence.

   f. Therefore, don't worry because there is nothing to worry about.
   g. Therefore, there's nothing to worry about.
   h. Therefore, nothing worries.
   j. Therefore, there's nothing don't worry.

9. Choose the correct way to write sentence 18.

   I'm so bored!

   a. i'm so bored!
   b. Am so bored!
   c. I'm so boring!
   d. No change is needed.

10. Gina wants to add this sentence to the paragraph that begins with sentence 15.

    There is thunder and lightning.

    Where would the sentence **best** fit?

    f. right after sentence 15
    g. right after sentence 16
    h. right after sentence 18
    j. right after sentence 17

11. Choose the correct way to write the underlined part of sentence 10.

The air traffic controllers are checking the <u>flite</u> plan.

   a. fight
   b. flight
   c. fleight
   d. No change is needed.

Trisha is in the third grade. Her class is learning about United States history. Her teacher asked each student to write about the history of the place where he or she was born. Trisha was born in Richmond, Virginia. She took notes and wrote her rough draft. Now she needs your help editing and revising it.

Here is Trisha's rough draft. Read it and then answer questions 1–10.

---

(1) I was born in <u>Richmond Virginia.</u> (2) Richmond is the capital of Virginia. (3) The <u>algonquian native americans</u> were some of the first people there. (4) Then in 1609, Captain John Smith bought land from the native Chief Powhatan and he, Chief Powhatan, was the father of the famous princess, Pocahontas. (5) The land that Captain Smith bought later became the <u>city</u> of Richmond. (6) Pretty soon, <u>it was pretty big and busy.</u>

(7) There are some interesting places in Richmond. (8) <u>Richard Randolph builds</u> Saint John's Church in 1741. (9) <u>They are one</u> of the oldest buildings in the state. (10) This church is where Patrick Henry said the famous words, "Give me liberty, or give me death!" (11) People like to visit the plantations and take canal boat tours. (12) The Virginia Museum of Fine Arts has art from ancient times and modern times.

(13) Up until 1779, Richmond was not the capital of Virginia. (14) Williamsburg was the first capital of Virginia. (15) Then Richmond became the capital of Virginia because it was in a better place. (16) The <u>guverner</u> works there now.

---

1. Choose the correct way to write the underlined part of sentence 1.

   I was born in <u>Richmond Virginia.</u>

   a. Richmond Virginia,
   b. Richmond, Virginia,
   c. Richmond, Virginia.
   d. No change is needed.

2. Read sentence 4. It is poorly written.

   Then in 1609, Captain John Smith bought land from the native Chief Powhatan and he, Chief Powhatan, was the father of the famous princess, Pocahontas.

   Choose the **best** way to rewrite this sentence.

   f. Then in 1609, Captain John Smith bought land from the native Chief Powhatan, the father of the famous princess, Pocahontas.
   g. Then in 1609, Captain John Smith bought land from the native Chief Powhatan. He, Chief Powhatan, was the father of the famous princess, Pocahontas.
   h. Then in 1609, Captain John Smith bought land from the native Chief Powhatan. Chief Powhatan, was the father of the famous princess, Pocahontas.
   j. Then in 1609, Captain John Smith bought land from the native Chief Powhatan and he was the father of the famous princess, Pocahontas.

3. Choose the correct way to write the underlined part of sentence 3.

   The <u>algonquian native americans</u> were some of the first people there.

   a. algonquian Native Americans
   b. Algonquian native americans
   c. Algonquian Native Americans
   d. No change is needed.

4. Trisha wants to change sentence 6 so that it is more specific.

   Pretty soon, <u>it was pretty big and busy.</u>

   Choose the **best** way to rewrite the underlined part of the sentence.

   f. there were a lot of people living there and working.
   g. it became the center of government and trade.
   h. it was a big city.
   j. a lot of people moved there.

5. Choose the correct way to write the underlined part of sentence 5.

   The land that Captain Smith bought later became the <u>city</u> of Richmond.

   a. City
   b. Cities
   c. Citys
   d. No change is needed.

6. Read sentence 12. It is poorly written.

   The Virginia Museum of Fine Arts has art from ancient times and modern times.

   Choose the **best** way to rewrite the sentence so that it does not repeat ideas.

   f. The Virginia Museum of Fine Arts has art from ancient times. It also has art from modern times.
   g. The Virginia Museum of Fine Arts has art from ancient times and from modern times.
   h. The Virginia Museum of Fine Arts has art from both ancient and modern times.
   j. The Virginia Museum of Fine Arts is ancient and modern.

7. Choose the correct way to write the underlined part of sentence 8.

   <u>Richard Randolph builds</u> Saint John's Church in 1741.

   a. Richard Randolph built
   b. Richard Randolph building
   c. Richard Randolph will build
   d. No change is needed.

8. Choose the correct way to write sentence 9.

   <u>They are one</u> of the oldest buildings in the state.

   f. We are one
   g. He is one
   h. It is one
   j. No change is needed.

9. Trisha wants to add this sentence to the paragraph that begins with sentence 13.

   It's been that way ever since.

   Where would the sentence **best** fit?

   a. right after sentence 14
   b. right after sentence 13
   c. right after sentence 16
   d. right after sentence 15

10. Choose the correct way to write the underlined part of sentence 16.

   The <u>guverner</u> works there now.

   f. guvernor
   g. governor
   h. governer
   j. No change is needed.

64

Sara's third-grade class is studying birds. Her teacher asked each student to choose one bird to write about. Sara chose the osprey. She organized her notes and wrote her rough draft. Now she needs your help editing and revising it.

Here is Sara's rough draft. Read it and then answer questions 1–11.

(1) If you go to the beach, you might see an osprey. (2) Sometimes people think these birds are sea gulls. (3) That's because their wings are <u>long and narrow, two.</u> (4) <u>There aren't any</u> ospreys around in the winter, except in parts of Texas and Florida. (5) Ospreys from the north migrate to South America. (6) My aunt went to South America last year for her vacation.

(7) The name, "osprey," means "fish hawk." (8) Ospreys are fish-eating raptors. (9) <u>Raptor are birds</u> of prey. (10) They do good diving. (11) They can dive from a hundred feet up in the air! (12) They put their wings together and drop straight down. (13) Sometimes they go underwater. (14) <u>They grabbed the fish</u> with their long claws. (15) Sometimes just fly down close to the water. (16) They can scoop out fish with their beaks. (17) They do this by using their beaks like buckets.

(18) Ospreys make nests out of wood, bones, and seaweed. (19) They build <u>the larger nests</u> in the country. (20) They lay three eggs in <u>April or May.</u> (21) In five weeks, the babies hatch.

1. Choose the correct way to write the underlined part of sentence 3.

    That's because their wings are <u>long and narrow, two.</u>

    a. long and narrow, to.
    b. long and narrow, too.
    c. too long and narrow.
    d. No change is needed.

2. Choose the sentence that does **not** belong in the paragraph that begins with sentence 1.

    f. sentence 5
    g. sentence 2
    h. sentence 1
    j. sentence 6

3. Choose the correct way to write the underlined part of sentence 9.

<u>Raptor are birds</u> of prey.

    a. A raptor are birds
    b. Raptors are birds
    c. Raptor are birds
    d. No change is needed.

4. Sara wants to add this sentence to the paragraph that begins with sentence 18.

Baby ospreys are very cute!

Where would the sentence **best** fit?

    f. right after sentence 21
    g. right after sentence 18
    h. right after sentence 20
    j. right after sentence 19

5. Choose the correct way to write the underlined part of sentence 4.

<u>There aren't any</u> ospreys around in the winter, except in parts of Texas and Florida.

    a. There isn't any
    b. There wasn't any
    c. There are any
    d. No change is needed.

6. Read sentence 10. It is poorly written.

    They do good diving.

    Choose the **best** way to rewrite this sentence.

    f. They are divers who are good.
    g. They dive good.
    h. They are good divers.
    j. They are diving good.

7. Choose the correct way to write the underlined part of sentence 14.

    <u>They grabbed the fish</u> with their long claws.

    a. They grab the fish
    b. They were grabbing the fish
    c. They would grab the fish
    d. No change is needed.

8. Choose the **best** way to combine the ideas in sentences 16 and 17 into one sentence.

    They can scoop out fish with their beaks. They do this by using their beaks like buckets.

    f. They can scoop out fish with buckets on their beaks.
    g. They can scoop out fish by using their beaks like buckets.
    h. They can scoop out buckets of fish.
    j. They can scoop out fish by using their beaks and buckets.

9. Choose the correct way to write the underlined part of sentence 19.

   They build <u>the larger nests</u> in the country.

   a. the most large nests
   b. the more larger nests
   c. the largest nests
   d. No change is needed.

10. Read sentence 15. It is poorly written.

    Sometimes just fly down close to the water.

    Choose the **best** way to rewrite this sentence.

    f. Sometimes they just fly down close to the water.
    g. Sometimes just fly right down close to the water.
    h. They just fly down close to the water sometimes.
    j. Sometimes just fly down close and to the water.

11. Choose the correct way to write the underlined part of sentence 20.

    They lay three eggs in <u>April or May.</u>

    a. april or May.
    b. April or may.
    c. april or may.
    d. No change is needed.

Morgan's third-grade class is planning to go on a nature walk. Her teacher asked each student to write a report about something that grows in the woods. Morgan chose to write about trees. She wrote her rough draft. Now she needs help editing and revising it.

Here is Morgan's rough draft. Read it and then answer questions 1–11.

(1) We have many trees in the United States. (2) They come in all shapes and sizes. (3) Here is what I learned about trees it's so cool.

(4) Trees come in two main types: broad-leaved trees and conifers. (5) In the eastern part of North America, there are mostly broad-leaved trees. (6) They can change their colors in the fall. (7) Their leaves get lost and they go to sleep in the winter. (8) Conifers live in colder places. (9) They have sharp needles instead of leaves. (10) They are called evergreens, and they don't lose their leaves in the fall. (11) Conifers make hard cones to protect <u>there seeds.</u>

(12) Did you know that you can use a pine cone to predict <u>the weather.</u> (13) You can! (14) When it's nice out, the <u>cones</u> scales are open. (15) When a storm is coming, the cone closes up. (16) The tree wants <u>to keep his seeds nice and dry.</u>

(17) One half of a tree is invisible to us. (18) That's because it's underground. (19) <u>Roots go</u> very far. (20) Some roots are as long as the tree is high! (21) If you have a tree that is one hundred and fifty feet tall, the roots could cover a soccer field. (22) It wonder that trees in the forest have enough room!

(23) <u>On friday,</u> we will see many trees on our nature walk. (24) I look forward to learning even more about them. (25) Also, the teachers are going to serve us pizza after! (26) I love learning about trees now!

1. Choose the correct way to write the underlined part of sentence 11.

   Conifers make hard cones to protect <u>there seeds.</u>

   a. they're seeds.
   b. they seeds.
   c. their seeds.
   d. No change is needed.

2. Choose the topic sentence for the paragraph that begins with sentence 17.

    f. It wonder that trees in the forest have enough room!

    g. If you have a tree that is one hundred and fifty feet tall, the roots could cover a soccer field.

    h. One half of a tree is invisible to us.

    j. That's because it's underground.

3. Choose the correct way to write the underlined part of sentence 12.

    Did you know that you can use a pine cone to predict <u>the weather.</u>

    a. the weather!

    b. the weather?

    c. the weather,

    d. No change is needed.

4. Read sentence 22. It is poorly written.

    It wonder that trees in the forest have enough room!

    Choose the **best** way to rewrite this sentence.

    f. It a wonder that trees in the forest have enough room!

    g. It's wonder that trees in the forest have enough room!

    h. It is wonder that trees in the forest have enough room!

    j. It's a wonder that trees in the forest have enough room!

70

5. Choose the correct way to write the underlined part of sentence 14.

   When it's nice out, the <u>cones</u> scales are open.

   a. cone's
   b. cone
   c. cones'
   d. No change is needed.

6. Read sentence 7. It is poorly written.

   Their leaves get lost and they go to sleep in the winter.

   Choose the **best** way to rewrite this sentence.

   f. They lost their leaves they go to sleep in the winter.
   g. Their leaves get lost and go to sleep in the winter.
   h. Leaves fall and they go to sleep in the winter.
   j. They lose their leaves and go to sleep in the winter.

7. Choose the correct way to write the underlined part of sentence 16.

   The tree wants <u>to keep his seeds nice and dry.</u>

   a. to keep our seeds nice and dry.
   b. to keep their seeds nice and dry.
   c. to keep its seeds nice and dry.
   d. No change is needed.

8. Read sentence 3. It is poorly written.

   Here is what I learned about trees it's so cool.

   Choose the **best** way to rewrite this sentence.

   f. Here is what I learned about trees. It's so cool.
   g. Here is what I learned about trees it is so cool.
   h. Here is what I learned about cool trees.
   j. Here is what I learned about trees, it's so cool.

9. Choose the correct way to write the underlined part of sentence 19.

   <u>Roots go</u> very far.

   a. Roots going
   b. Roots does go
   c. Roots are going
   d. No change is needed.

10. Choose the sentence that does **not** belong in the paragraph that begins with sentence 23.

   f. sentence 24
   g. sentence 25
   h. sentence 23
   j. sentence 26

11. Choose the correct way to write the underlined part of sentence 23.

   <u>On friday,</u> we will see many trees on our nature walk.

   a. On Friday,
   b. on friday,
   c. on Friday
   d. No change is needed.

Solomon's third-grade teacher asked each student to write a letter to a friend. Solomon decided to write about billiards. He listed his ideas and wrote his rough draft. Now he needs your help editing and revising it.

Here is Solomon's rough draft. Read it and then answer questions 1–10.

(1) Dear Phil,

(2) Guess what! (3) I just got a new game table it is amazing. (4) You can play a lot of different games. (5) It works great <u>wether</u> you play air hockey or table tennis. (6) My favorite is billiards. (7) Billiards that's the same thing pool. (8) Another game I love is chess.

(9) Billiards is so much fun! (10) You have to get the balls into the pockets. (11) You have to hit the cue ball, though. (12) You hit it with your cue stick. (13) Then the cue ball <u>nox</u> into the ball you want. (14) Whatever you do, do not hit the eight ball into any pockets. (15) If you do. (16) You lose!

(17) <u>You wanna come over</u> Saturday and try out my new game table? (18) You can learn how to play billiards. (19) Bring your dog so he can <u>play with Buster.</u>

(20) Your friend

(21) Solomon

1. Choose the correct way to write the underlined part of sentence 5.

   It works great <u>wether</u> you play air hockey or table tennis.

   a. whether
   b. weather
   c. wheather
   d. No change is needed.

73

2. Read sentence 3. It is poorly written.

   I just got a new game table it is amazing.

   Choose the **best** way to rewrite this sentence.

   f. I just got a new game table that it is amazing!
   g. I just got a new game table, it is amazing!
   h. I just got a new game table It is amazing!
   j. I just got a new game table. It is amazing!

3. Choose the correct way to write the underlined part of sentence 17.

   <u>You wanna come over</u> Saturday and try out my new game table?

   a. Wants to come over
   b. You want come over
   c. Do you want to come over on
   d. No change is needed.

4. Choose the sentence that does **not** belong in the paragraph that begins with sentence 2.

   f. sentence 8
   g. sentence 3
   h. sentence 2
   j. sentence 6

5. Choose the correct way to write the underlined part of sentence 19.

   Bring your dog so he can <u>play with Buster.</u>

   a. playing with Buster.
   b. will play with Buster.
   c. played with Buster.
   d. No change is needed.

6. Read sentence 7. It is poorly written.

   Billiards that's the same thing pool.

   Choose the **best** way to rewrite this sentence.

   f. Billiards is the same thing as pool.
   g. Billiards is that which is pool.
   h. That's the same things as is pool.
   j. That's billiards or pool.

7. Choose the correct way to write line 20, the closing of the letter.

   Your friend

   a. your friend
   b. Your friend,
   c. Your Friend,
   d. No change is needed.

8. Choose the **best** way to combine the ideas in sentences 15 and 16 into one sentence.

> **If you do. You lose!**

f. If you do. You do lose!
g. If you lose!
h. If you do lose!
j. If you do, you lose!

9. Choose the correct way to write the underlined part of sentence 13.

> **Then the cue ball <u>nox</u> into the ball you want.**

a. nocks
b. knox
c. knocks
d. No change is needed.

10. Solomon wants to add this sentence to the paragraph that begins with sentence 9.

> **It's okay, though, because if you lose you can just play again!**

Where would the sentence **best** fit?

f. right after sentence 14
g. right after sentence 15
h. right after sentence 16
j. right after sentence 9

Sierra is in the third grade. Her class is planning to visit a space museum. Sierra's teacher asked the students in the class to choose one astronaut and to write about him or her. Sierra has written her rough draft, and now she needs your help editing and revising it.

Here is Sierra's rough draft. Read it and then answer questions 1–10.

(1) Sally Ride was the <u>first american woman</u> to travel in space. (2) She was born in 1951 in <u>Los Angeles California.</u> (3) She studied science, and then she <u>became a astronaut.</u> (4) She rode in the space shuttle, *Challenger*, in 1983. (5) The flight was six long.

(6) Sally Ride did some important things on the shuttle. (7) She helped release <u>satellites She</u> did some experiments in space. (8) My father and I did an experiment for my science project last month. (9) Sally Ride was a good scientist.

(10) There was a very bad accident on <u>January 28 1986.</u> (11) The *Challenger* took off, but right after that. (12) It broke apart. (13) All seven people aboard died. (14) It was a national tragedy. (15) The whole country mourned the loss of the brave astronauts. (16) Sally Ride <u>helped to know why.</u>

(17) Sally Ride <u>doesn't travel</u> in space anymore. (18) She is a science teacher in California.

(19) At the space museum, I'm going to pretend that I'm Sally Ride!

1. Choose the correct way to write the underlined part of sentence 1.

   Sally Ride was the <u>first american woman</u> to travel in space.

   a. first American woman
   b. First American Woman
   c. first american Woman
   d. No change is needed.

2. Read sentence 5. It is poorly written.

   The flight was six long.

   Choose the **best** way to rewrite this sentence.

   f. The flight was long six.
   g. The flight was as long as six.
   h. The flight was six days long.
   j. The flight was six years long.

3. Choose the correct way to write the underlined part of sentence 2.

   She was born in 1951 in <u>Los Angeles California.</u>

   a. Los, Angeles, California.
   b. Los, Angeles California.
   c. Los Angeles, California.
   d. No change is needed.

4. Sierra wants to change sentence 16 so that it is more specific.

   Sally Ride <u>helped to know why.</u>

   Choose the **best** way to rewrite the underlined part of the sentence.

   f. helped.
   g. helped scientists try to find out what had gone wrong.
   h. helped find out why it had happened?
   j. helped them all find out why.

78

5. Choose the correct way to write the underlined part of sentence 3.

   She studied science, and then she <u>became a astronaut.</u>

   a. became an astronaut.
   b. became astronaut.
   c. became some astronaut.
   d. No change is needed.

6. Choose the sentence that does **not** belong in the paragraph that begins with sentence 6.

   f. sentence 9
   g. sentence 7
   h. sentence 8
   j. sentence 6

7. Choose the correct way to write the underlined part of sentence 7.

   She helped release <u>satellites She</u> did some experiments in space.

   a. satellites, she
   b. satellites. She
   c. satellites? She
   d. No change is needed.

8. Choose the correct way to write the underlined part of sentence 10.

   There was a very bad accident on <u>January 28 1986.</u>

   f. January, 28, 1986.
   g. January 28, 1986.
   h. January, 28. 1986.
   j. No change is needed.

9. Sierra wants to add this sentence to the paragraph that begins with sentence 1, the paragraph that begins with sentence 17, or the paragraph that begins with sentence 19.

   That's because someday I want to be an astronaut just like her!

   Where would the sentence **best** fit?

   a. right after sentence 1
   b. right after sentence 4
   c. right after sentence 18
   d. right after sentence 19

10. Choose the correct way to write the underlined part of sentence 17.

    Sally Ride <u>doesn't travel</u> in space anymore.

    f. don't travel
    g. didn't travel
    h. wasn't traveling
    j. No change is needed.

Jasmine's third-grade class is planning to go bird watching. Her teacher asked each student to get ready for the trip by writing a report about birds. Jasmine wrote a rough draft, but now she needs your help to edit and revise her work.

Here is Jasmine's rough draft. Read it and then answer questions 1–10.

(1) Birds are amazing. (2) They are the <u>prettyest</u> creatures, and they can fly. (3) Let me tell you why birds are so special. (4) Let me tell you why birds are so interesting.

(5) Everybody knows that birds can fly because they have wings. (6) Did you know that they also have very light skeletons? (7) Many of <u>there bones</u> are hollow. (8) This also helps them to fly. (9) Imagine. (10) A bird with heavy bones.

(11) People lose hair all the time. (12) News replace the lost. (13) Birds don't have hair, but they lose their feathers. (14) <u>When an old feather fall out,</u> a new one grows to replace it.

(15) Birds lay eggs and care for their young. (16) The parents build nests in some interesting places. (17) For example, <u>the weaverbird builds</u> a nest with a leaf of a tree. (18) It sews together the edges of the leaf. (19) Then, the leaf holds the tiny nest. (20) Birds like to build nests in places that are hard to find. (21) <u>He is safer</u> that way.

(22) In the fall, some birds migrate to warmer places. (23) Not all kinds of birds migrate. (24) The ruffed grouse stays in the same place all year. (25) Some geese migrate, but some stay behind. (26) Many hawks migrate through this area. (27) I saw a hawk fly over my garden yesterday!

(28) I hope we see many birds on our bird-watching trip. (29) I am looking forward to it!

1. Choose the correct way to write the underlined part of sentence 2.

   They are the <u>prettyest</u> creatures, and they can fly.

   a. prittiest
   b. prittyest
   c. prettiest
   d. No change is needed.

2. Choose the **best** way to combine the ideas in sentences 3 and 4 into one sentence.

> **Let me tell you why birds are so special. Let me tell you why birds are so interesting**.

    f. Let me tell you why birds are so special and also let me tell you why birds are so interesting.

    g. Let me tell you why birds are so special. And interesting.

    h. Let me tell you why birds are so special and why they are so interesting.

    j. Let me tell you why birds are so special and interesting.

3. Choose the correct way to write the underlined part of sentence 7.

> **Many of <u>there bones</u> are hollow.**

    a. they're bones

    b. they's bones

    c. their bones

    d. No change is needed.

4. Choose the topic sentence of this composition.

    f. Birds are amazing.

    g. Birds don't have hair, but they lose their feathers.

    h. Birds lay eggs and care for their young.

    j. I am looking forward to it!

5. Choose the sentence that is a good supporting detail about birds.

    a. Birds lay eggs and care for their young.

    b. People lose hair all the time.

    c. I am looking forward to it!

    d. He is safer that way

6. Choose the correct way to write the underlined part of sentence 14.

   When an old feather fall out, a new one grows to replace it.

   f. When an old feather falling out,
   g. When an old feather falls out,
   h. When an old feather it falls out,
   j. No change is needed.

7. Choose the correct way to write the underlined part of sentence 17.

   For example, the weaverbird builds a nest with a leaf of a tree.

   a. the weaverbird build
   b. the weaverbird building
   c. the weaverbird built
   d. No change is needed.

8. Read sentence 12. It is poorly written.

   News replace the lost.

   Choose the **best** way to rewrite this sentence.

   f. The news replaces the lost.
   g. New ones replace the ones that have been lost.
   h. Replacements are made.
   j. New replaces old.

83

9. Choose the **best** way to combine the ideas in sentences 9 and 10 into one sentence.

> **Imagine. A bird with heavy bones.**

    a. Can you imagining a bird with heavy bones?
    b. Can you imagine a bird with heavy bones?
    c. Are you imagining a bird with heavy bones?
    d. Imagine heavy bones.

10. Choose the correct way to write the underlined part of sentence 21.

> **<u>He is safer</u> that way.**

    f. I am safer
    g. You are safer
    h. They are safer
    j. No change is needed.

Grace is in the third grade. Her class is studying camouflage. Her teacher asked each student in the class to choose a habitat and to write about the camouflage that animals use there. Grace chose the ocean. She took notes from two books, and she wrote a rough draft. Now she needs your help to edit and revise her work.

Here is Grace's rough draft. Read it and then answer questions 1–10.

(1) "Camouflage" means "to hide something by making it look like its surroundings." (2) Many ocean animals <u>used</u> camouflage. (3) To hide.

(4) The <u>leafy sea dragon</u> uses camouflage. (5) It is no ordinary seahorse its fins look just like seaweed. (6) Maybe you can guess where the leafy sea dragon lives. (7) It lives in the seaweed, of course!

(8) Next time you find a shell at the beach, take a close look. (9) There a crab could be on it. (10) Some crabs are the same color as shells. (11) The flounder uses color, too. (12) <u>Its hides</u> in the sand on the ocean floor. (13) It makes itself look like sand and pebbles.

(14) <u>Some fish gives</u> off light. (15) They look like they are glowing. (16) That helps the fish to hide in <u>patchs</u> of sunlight.

1. Which one of these is **not** a complete sentence?

   a. To hide.
   b. The <u>leafy sea dragon</u> uses camouflage.
   c. The flounder uses color, too.
   d. They look like they are glowing.

2. Choose the correct way to write the underlined part of sentence 2.

   Many ocean animals <u>used</u> camouflage.

   f. will use
   g. use
   h. were using
   j. No change is needed.

3. Read sentence 5. It is poorly written.

   It is no ordinary seahorse its fins look just like seaweed.

   Choose the **best** way to rewrite this sentence.

   a. It is not ordinary. Just like seaweed.
   b. It is no ordinary seahorse. It has seaweed for fins.
   c. It is no ordinary seahorse. Its fins look just like seaweed.
   d. It is an ordinary seahorse. Its fins look just like seaweed.

4. Choose the correct way to write the underlined part of sentence 4.

   The <u>leafy sea dragon</u> uses camouflage.

   f. Leafy sea dragon
   g. leafy Sea Dragon
   h. leafy Sea dragon
   j. No change is needed.

5. Read sentence 9. It is poorly written.

   There a crab could be on it.

   Choose the **best** way to rewrite this sentence.

   a. There is a crab on it.
   b. There could be a crab on it.
   c. There is no crab on it.
   d. There could not be a crab on it.

6. Choose the correct way to write the underlined part of sentence 16.

That helps the fish to hide in <u>patchs</u> of sunlight.

f. paches
g. patches
h. patchess
j. were using

7. Choose the **best** way to combine the ideas in sentences 14 and 15 into one sentence.

<u>Some fish gives</u> off light. They look like they are glowing.

a. Some fish give off light some fish look like they are glowing.
b. Some fish giving off light, looking like they are glowing.
c. Some fish look like they are glowing because they give off light.
d. Some fish, they look like they are glowing, they give off light.

8. Choose the correct way to write the underlined part of sentence 12.

<u>Its hides</u> in the sand on the ocean floor.

f. It's hides
g. It hides
h. It is hides
j. No change is needed.

9. Grace wants to add this sentence to the paragraph that begins with sentence 14.

   For example, the hatchetfish is decorated with light.

   Where would the sentence **best** fit?

   a. right after sentence 16
   b. right after sentence 15
   c. right before sentence 14
   d. right after sentence 14

10. Choose the correct way to write the underlined part of sentence 14.

    <u>Some fish gives</u> off light.

    f. Some fishes give
    g. Some fish give
    h. Some fishes gives
    j. No change is needed.

Meena is in the third grade. Her class is studying the weather. Her teacher asked each student in the class to describe a storm. Meena decided to write about the Great Hurricane of 1938. She has written a rough draft, but now she needs your help to edit and revise it.

Here is Meena's rough draft. Read it and then answer questions 1–11.

(1) In 1938, a terrible thing happened to New England. (2) Have you ever heard of the Great Hurricane of '38?

(3) In 1938, <u>there was no</u> satellites or radar. (4) People couldn't get information on the <u>Internet or television or with their cell phones.</u> (5) There were no weather maps to look at.

(6) The hurricane started over the <u>atlantic ocean.</u> (7) The Weather Bureau told everyone not to worry. (8) They were wrong!

(9) When the hurricane hit New England. (10) People were not prepared. (11) They got caught in the storm. (12) It was a huge storm it was five hundred miles wide it had very strong winds. (13) The tide got higher up twenty-five feet more. (14) People's houses were <u>fluded.</u> (15) Some people had to climb. (16) They had to climb onto their roofs.

(17) This would not happen today. (18) Weather reports are more accurate. (19) If a hurricane is coming, <u>we knew</u> about it. (20) We will have time to prepare.

1. Meena wants to add this sentence to the paragraph that begins with sentence 3.

    People listened to the radio instead.

    Where would the sentence **best** fit?

    a. right after sentence 3
    b. right after sentence 4
    c. right after sentence 5
    d. right before sentence 3

2. Choose the correct way to write the underlined part of sentence 3.

In 1938, <u>there was no</u> satellites or radar.

   f. there were no
   g. there weren't no
   h. there are no
   j. No change is needed.

3. Which one of these is **not** a complete sentence?

   a. Have you ever heard of the Great Hurricane of '38?
   b. There were no weather maps to look at.
   c. They were wrong!
   d. When the hurricane hit New England.

4. Choose the correct way to write the underlined part of sentence 19.

If a hurricane is coming, <u>we knew</u> about it.

   f. we will be knowing
   g. we will know
   h. we were knowing
   j. No change is needed.

5. Meena wants to change sentence 12 so that it is more specific.

    It was a huge storm it was five hundred miles wide it had <u>very strong winds.</u>

    Choose the **best** way to rewrite the underlined part of the sentence.

    a. super-strong winds.
    b. winds blowing hard.
    c. the fastest winds.
    d. one hundred eighty mile-per-hour winds.

6. Choose the correct way to write the underlined part of sentence 6.

    The hurricane started over the <u>atlantic ocean.</u>

    f. atlantic Ocean.
    g. Atlantic ocean.
    h. Atlantic Ocean.
    j. No change is needed.

7. Read sentence 12. It is poorly written.

    It was a huge storm it was five hundred miles wide it had very strong winds.

    Choose the **best** way to rewrite this sentence.

    a. The huge storm was five hundred miles wide with very strong winds.
    b. It was a huge storm with five hundred miles and strong winds.
    c. It was a huge storm. Five hundred miles wide. Very strong winds.
    d. It was a huge storm. And very wide, strong winds.

91

8. Choose the correct way to write the underlined part of sentence 14.

   People's houses were <u>fluded.</u>

   f. fludded.
   g. flooded.
   h. flodded.
   j. No change is needed.

9. Read sentence 13. It is poorly written.

   The tide got higher up twenty-five feet more.

   Choose the **best** way to rewrite this sentence.

   a. The tide rose twenty-five feet higher than usual.
   b. The tide got twenty-five feet.
   c. The tide rose higher, twenty-five feet more higher.
   d. The tide. It got twenty-five feet higher.

10. Choose the correct way to write the underlined part of sentence 4.

    People couldn't get information on the <u>Internet or television or with their cell phones.</u>

    f. Internet television or with their cell phones.
    g. Internet, and/or television and/or with their cell phones.
    h. Internet, television, or with their cell phones.
    j. No change is needed.

92

11. Choose the **best** way to combine the ideas in sentences 15 and 16 into one sentence.

> **Some people had to climb. They had to climb onto their roofs.**

   a. Some people had to climb, climbing onto their roofs.
   b. Some people had to climb onto their roofs.
   c. Some people, they had to climb onto their roofs.
   d. Some people had to climb they climbed onto their roofs.

Diana's third-grade class is learning about China. Her teacher asked each student to choose a topic related to China and to write a report. Diana chose to write about food. She took notes at the library and wrote her rough draft. Now she needs help editing and revising it.

Here is Diana's rough draft. Read it and then answer questions 1–10.

(1) China is a huge country in <u>eastern Asia.</u> (2) <u>One-fifth of the world's people</u> live there. (3) They eat many kinds of food.

(4) In the south. (5) People eat a lot of rice. (6) In the north, they eat more wheat. (7) They use the wheat. (8) They make noodles and bread. (9) Chinese people <u>like to eating</u> vegetables. (10) Chinese people like to eat cabbage especially. (11) They eat a lot of tofu, too. (12) They like best for meat pork and chicken. (13) Duck is very <u>poplar</u> in the north.

(14) Breakfast is rice or <u>soup.</u> (15) People don't usually eat with forks and knives. (16) They use chopsticks and soup spoons. (17) Their favorite drink is tea.

1. Which one of these is **not** a complete sentence?

   a. They eat many kinds of food.
   b. In the south.
   c. People eat a lot of rice.
   d. They use the wheat.

2. Choose the correct way to write the underlined part of sentence 1.

   China is a huge country in <u>eastern Asia.</u>

   f. Eastern Asia.
   g. Eastern asia.
   h. eastern asia.
   j. No change is needed.

94

3. Choose the **best** way to combine the ideas in sentences 7 and 8 into one sentence.

   They use the wheat. They make noodles and bread.

   a. They use the wheat, and they use noodles and bread, too.
   b. They use the wheat made out of bread and noodles.
   c. They use the wheat, noodles, and bread.
   d. They use the wheat to make noodles and bread.

4. Choose the correct way to write the underlined part of sentence 2.

   <u>One-fifth of the world's people</u> live there.

   f. One-fifth of the world of people
   g. One-fifth of the worlds's people
   h. One-fifth of the worlds' people
   j. No change is needed.

5. Choose the correct way to write the underlined part of sentence 9.

   Chinese people <u>like to eating</u> vegetables.

   a. like to ate
   b. like to be eating
   c. like to eat
   d. No change is needed.

95

6. Choose the correct way to write the underlined part of sentence 13.

   Duck is very <u>poplar</u> in the north.

   f. popular
   g. popyular
   h. poppular
   j. No change is needed.

7. Diana wants to add this sentence to the paragraph that begins with sentence 4.

   Tofu is made from soybeans.

   Where would the sentence **best** fit?

   a. right after sentence 5
   b. right after sentence 10
   c. right after sentence 11
   d. right after sentence 12

8. Choose the **best** way to combine the ideas in sentences 9 and 10 into one sentence.

   Chinese people <u>like to eating</u> vegetables. Chinese people like to eat cabbage especially.

   f. Chinese people like to eat vegetables, and Chinese people like cabbage especially.
   g. Chinese people like to eat vegetables, especially cabbage.
   h. Chinese people like vegetables, and Chinese people like cabbage a lot.
   j. Chinese people like to eat vegetables, the Chinese like to eat cabbage.

96

9. Read sentence 12. It is poorly written.

They like best for meat pork and chicken.

Choose the **best** way to rewrite this sentence.

a. They best for meat like pork and chicken.
b. For meat, they like pork and chicken the best.
c. For the best, they like pork and chicken for meat.
d. For pork and chicken they like the best meat.

10. Diana wants to change sentence 14 so that it is more specific.

Breakfast is rice or <u>soup.</u>

Choose the **best** way to rewrite the underlined part of sentence.

f. a bowl of soup.
g. chicken noodle soup.
h. a little bit of soup.
j. sometimes soup.

97

Ryan is in the third grade. His class is learning about dinosaurs. His teacher asked each student to pretend that he or she was a dinosaur. The teacher told the students to describe themselves and their behavior as if they were dinosaurs. Ryan wrote his rough draft, but now he needs your help editing and revising it.

Here is Ryan's rough draft. Read it and then answer questions 1–11.

(1) My name is Stego. (2) I am a stegosaurus. (3) I live in the Cretaceous period. (4) In one hundred forty million years, this place will be Colorado. (5) Have you ever been to Colorado? (6) By then <u>I'll be gone.</u>

(7) I am a huge dinosaur. (8) I am thirty feet long. (9) I have big pointy plates down my back. (10) Don't worry I won't eat you I am a herbivore that means I only eat plants. (11) I have short little legs. (12) <u>my head</u> is down near the ground. (13) That's why I eat moss and ferns. (14) Because are short.

(15) It's cold out <u>hear!</u> (16) It's time to warm up. (17) I'll just turn my bony plates toward the sun. (18) Ah, that's nice.

(19) Uh-oh! (20) Here comes a sharp-toothed dinosaur. (21) I'll hit him with my <u>spikked</u> tail. (22) My tail is a weapon. (23) There! (24) Now <u>its safe</u> for lunch.

1. Choose the sentence that does **not** belong in the paragraph that begins with sentence 1.

    a. sentence 1
    b. sentence 5
    c. sentence 6
    d. sentence 2

2. Choose the correct way to write the underlined part of sentence 6.

    By then <u>I'll be gone.</u>

    f. I was gone.
    g. I will be gone.
    h. I am gone.
    j. No change is needed.

3. Choose the **best** way to combine the ideas in sentences 7 and 8 into one sentence.

I am a huge dinosaur. I am thirty feet long.

a. I am a huge dinosaur, thirty long feet.
b. I am a huge dinosaur with thirty feet.
c. I am a huge dinosaur; I am a long dinosaur, too.
d. I am a huge thirty-foot-long dinosaur.

4. Choose the correct way to write the underlined part of sentence 24.

Now <u>its safe</u> for lunch.

f. it's safe
g. its's safe
h. its' safe
j. No change is needed.

5. Read sentence 10. It is poorly written.

Don't worry I won't eat you I am a herbivore that means I only eat plants.

Choose the **best** way to rewrite this sentence.

a. Don't worry because I won't eat you and I am a herbivore that means I only eat plants.
b. Don't worry! I won't eat you I am a herbivore. That means I only eat plants.
c. Don't worry! I won't eat you. I am a herbivore, and that means I only eat plants.
d. Don't worry because I won't eat you, so I am a herbivore, so that means I only eat plants.

6. Choose the correct way to write the underlined part of sentence 12.

   <u>my head</u> is down near the ground.

   f. my Head
   g. my heads
   h. My head
   j. No change is needed.

7. Which one of these is **not** a complete sentence?

   a. Have you ever been to Colorado?
   b. Because are short.
   c. It's time to warm up.
   d. Ah, that's nice.

8. Choose the correct way to write the underlined part of sentence 21.

   I'll hit him with my <u>spikked</u> tail.

   f. spicked
   g. spiked
   h. sbiked
   j. No change is needed.

100

9. Choose the sentence that **best** fits right after sentence 22.

    a. I feel warmer now.
    b. Some stegosauruses lived in what is now India.
    c. The spikes are three feet long!
    d. I don't have any teeth.

10. Choose the correct way to write the underlined part of sentence 15.

    It's cold out <u>hear!</u>

    f. heer!
    g. heir!
    h. here!
    j. No change is needed.

11. Ryan wants to change sentence 22 so that it is more specific.

    My tail is <u>a weapon.</u>

    Choose the **best** way to rewrite the underlined part of the sentence.

    a. a sharp and dangerous weapon.
    b. a good weapon.
    c. the kind of weapon that can hurt.
    d. sharp.

Katie's third-grade class is learning how to write letters. Her teacher asked each student to write a letter telling a friend about the class trip to the fire station. Katie wrote her rough draft, and now she needs help editing and revising it.

Here is Katie's rough draft. Read it and then answer questions 1–10.

(1) Dear Chris,

(2) Yesterday my class went to the fire station. (3) I had never gone <u>to an fire station</u> before. (4) It <u>will be</u> so interesting.

(5) The firefighters talked to us about safety. (6) They said never to play with fire. (7) Never play with matches and never play with candles. (8) Kids set one hundred thousand fires every year that causes damage. (9) Make sure there are smoke alarms in your house. (10) <u>You're family</u> has to have a plan. (11) For when there is a fire.

(12) The firefighters showed us how they crawl on the floor in a fire. (13) If the room is <u>smokie,</u> get down and crawl. (14) They showed us how they use the extinguishers. (15) I got some of the white stuff on my foot. (16) It was fun.

(17) Love?

(18) Katie

1. Choose the topic sentence for the paragraph that begins with sentence 5.
    a. The firefighters talked to us about safety.
    b. Make sure there are smoke alarms in your house.
    c. Never play with matches and never play with candles.
    d. They said never to play with fire.

2. Choose the correct way to write the underlined part of sentence 4.

It <u>will be</u> so interesting.

    f. would be
    g. would have been
    h. was
    j. No change is needed.

3. Read sentence 7. It is poorly written.

Never play with matches and never play with candles.

Choose the **best** way to rewrite the sentence so that it does not repeat ideas.

    a. Never play with matches, never play with candles.
    b. Never play with matches or candles.
    c. Never play with matches, candles.
    d. Never play with candle matches.

4. Choose the correct way to write the underlined part of sentence 13.

If the room is <u>smokie,</u> get down and crawl.

    f. smokey,
    g. smokee,
    h. smoky,
    j. No change is needed.

5. Read sentence 8. It is poorly written.

   Kids set one hundred thousand fires every year that causes damage.

   Choose the **best** way to rewrite this sentence.

   a. Kids set one hundred thousand fires in the years that have damage.
   b. Every one hundred thousand years, kids set fires that cause damage.
   c. Every year, one hundred thousand kids set fires for damage.
   d. Every year, kids set one hundred thousand fires that cause damage.

6. Choose the correct way to write the underlined part of sentence 10.

   <u>You're family</u> has to have a plan.

   f. Yore family
   g. Your family
   h. Youre' family
   j. No change is needed.

7. Choose the sentence that **best** fits right after sentence 9.

   a. Make sure you know what to do.
   b. Ask a firefighter.
   c. Change the batteries every year.
   d. Make sure you are safe.

8. Choose the correct way to write line 17, the closing of the letter.

   Love?

   f. Love
   g. love,
   h. Love,
   j. No change is needed.

9. Which one of these is **not** a complete sentence?

   a. It will be so interesting.
   b. For when there is a fire.
   c. They said never to play with fire.
   d. It was fun.

10. Choose the correct way to write the underlined part of sentence 3.

    I had never gone <u>to an fire station</u> before.

    f. to a fire station
    g. to fire station
    h. to afire station
    j. No change is needed.

Antonio's third-grade class is learning about the artist, Pablo Picasso. His art teacher asked each student to look at Picasso's "The Old Guitarist" and to write a reaction paper. Antonio brainstormed his ideas using a graphic organizer. Then he wrote his rough draft, and he needs your help editing and revising it.

Here is Antonio's rough draft. Read it and then answer questions 1–11.

---

(1) "The Old Guitarist" makes me feel sad. (2) I think the man is <u>sad and tired and and lonely.</u> (3) He is all by himself and his head is hanging down his face is all wrinkled, his body is so long and skinny. (4) His mouth <u>looks sad, to.</u>

(5) <u>Their is</u> no sun in the sky. (6) There are no trees outside there are no birds outside. (7) The room is empty. (8) The man has no shoes on his feet. (9) I got a new pair of shoes yesterday. (10) The picture makes me feel empty.

(11) The painting has very sad colors. (12) Everything is blue, gray, or brown. (13) If Picasso put some red or yellow in there, it would look better.

(14) I think the man <u>will be playing</u> a sad song on the guitar. (15) Maybe he misses his friend. (16) When I look at this picture, I miss my <u>friend</u> who moved away. (17) Maybe Picasso missed somebody, too.

---

1. Read sentence 6. It is poorly written.

   There are no trees outside there are no birds outside.

   Choose the **best** way to rewrite the sentence.

   a. There are no trees or birds outside.
   b. There are no trees outside, but there are no birds outside.
   c. There are no trees, and there are no birds, outside.
   d. There are no outside trees or outside birds.

106

2. Choose the correct way to write the underlined part of sentence 16.

   When I look at this picture, I miss my <u>friend</u> who moved away.

   f. frend
   g. freind
   h. friennd
   j. No change is needed.

3. Choose the sentence that does **not** belong in the paragraph that begins with sentence 5.

   a. sentence 6
   b. sentence 9
   c. sentence 8
   d. sentence 7

4. Choose the correct way to write the underlined part of sentence 5.

   <u>Their is</u> no sun in the sky.

   f. They're is
   g. There is
   h. They are is
   j. No change is needed.

5. Choose the topic sentence for the paragraph that begins with sentence 5.

   a. The room is empty.
   b. I got a new pair of shoes yesterday.
   c. The man has no shoes on his feet.
   d. The picture makes me feel empty.

6. Choose the correct way to write the underlined part of sentence 4.

   His mouth <u>looks sad, to.</u>

   f. look sad, two.
   g. looks sad, too.
   h. too looks sad.
   j. No change is needed.

7. Read sentence 3. It is poorly written.

   **He is all by himself and his head is hanging down his
   face is all wrinkled, his body is so long and skinny.**

   Choose the **best** way to rewrite this sentence.

   a. He is all by himself. His head is hanging down. His face is all wrinkled.
      His body is so long. He is so skinny.
   b. He is all by himself, his head is hanging down, his face is all wrinkled, his
      body is so long, his body is so skinny.
   c. He is all by himself. His head is hanging down, and his face is all
      wrinkled. His body is so long and skinny.
   d. He is all by himself, and his head is hanging down, and his face is all
      wrinkled, and his body is so long and skinny.

8. Choose the correct way to write the underlined part of sentence 2.

   I think the man is <u>sad and tired and and lonely.</u>

   f. sad, and tired, and lonely.
   g. sad, tired, and lonely.
   h. sad, tired, lonely.
   j. No change is needed.

9. Choose the sentence that **best** fits right after sentence 12.

    a. Even the man's skin is blue.
    b. The man has a sad face.
    c. The man looks lonely.
    d. The man has a guitar.

10. Choose the correct way to write the underlined part of sentence 14.

    I think the man <u>will be playing</u> a sad song on the guitar.

    f. played
    g. would have been playing
    h. is playing
    j. No change is needed.

11. Antonio wants to change sentence 13 so that it is more specific.

    If Picasso put some red or yellow in there, <u>it would look better.</u>

    Choose the **best** way to rewrite the underlined part of the sentence.

    a. it would look nicer.
    b. it would look great.
    c. it would look more cheerful.
    d. it would look fine.

109

Dan's third-grade class visited a museum of natural history. His teacher asked the students to write a report about their favorite part of the museum. Dan decided to write about the Ice Age. He wrote his rough draft and now he needs your help editing and revising it.

Here is Dan's rough draft. Read it and then answer questions 1–11.

---

(1) My class <u>visits</u> a museum of natural history last week. (2) My favorite part of the museum was the Ice Age exhibit.

(3) First, we rode through a glacier on an escalator, and it looked real! (4) Then, we watched a <u>large globe spins around.</u> (5) There were lights on it. (6) They showed how much of the planet was covered with ice during the <u>Ice Age.</u>

(7) The northern part of our country was once covered with ice. (8) I like to go skating. (9) The glaciers moved south and covered the whole place. (10) Covering part of the Atlantic Ocean, too. (11) When the glaciers moved across the land, they pushed huge rocks. (12) You can see some of these rocks when you go hiking in the north. (13) If you see a rock that looks like a <u>gyent</u> dropped it there, a glacier probably pushed it.

(14) The museum was a fun place. (15) I learned a lot. (16) I hope I can go <u>they're</u> again soon!

---

1. Choose the topic sentence of this report.

    a. My favorite part of the museum was the Ice Age exhibit.
    b. First, we rode through the glacier on an escalator, and it looked real!
    c. The northern part of our country was once covered with ice.
    d. I learned a lot.

110

2. Choose the correct way to write the underlined part of sentence 1.

   My class <u>visits</u> a museum of natural history last week.

   f. will visit
   g. had visited
   h. visited
   j. No change is needed.

3. Read sentence 3. It is poorly written.

   First, we rode through a glacier on an escalator, and it looked real!

   Choose the correct way to rewrite this sentence.

   a. First, we rode an escalator. The glacier looked real!
   b. First, we rode on an escalator, and it looked real!
   c. First, we rode an escalator through a glacier that looked real!
   d. First, we rode an escalator. Through a glacier. The glacier looked real!

4. Choose the correct way to write the underlined part of sentence 13.

   If you see a rock that looks like a <u>gyent</u> dropped it there, a glacier probably pushed it.

   f. giant
   g. gient
   h. jyant
   j. No change is needed.

5. Choose the sentence that does **not** belong in the paragraph that begins with sentence 7.

    a. sentence 10
    b. sentence 8
    c. sentence 9
    d. sentence 7

6. Choose the correct way to write the underlined part of sentence 6.

    They showed how much of the planet was covered with ice during the <u>Ice Age.</u>

    f. ice age.
    g. ice Age.
    h. Ice age.
    j. No change is needed.

7. Dan wants to change sentence 9 so that it is more specific.

    The glaciers moved south and covered <u>the whole place.</u>

    Choose the **best** way to rewrite the underlined part of the sentence.

    a. the whole area.
    b. the northern United States.
    c. everywhere.
    d. the whole entire place.

8. Choose the correct way to write the underlined part of sentence 4.

   Then, we watched a <u>large globe spins around.</u>

   f. large globe spin around.
   g. large globe spun around.
   h. large globe spinning around.
   j. No change is needed.

9. Which one of these is **not** a complete sentence?

   a. There were lights on it.
   b. They showed how much of the planet was covered with ice during the Ice Age.
   c. Covering part of the Atlantic Ocean, too.
   d. You can see some of these rocks when you go hiking in the north.

10. Choose the correct way to write the underlined part of sentence 16.

    I hope I can go <u>they're</u> again soon!

    f. their
    g. there
    h. ther
    j. No change is needed.

11. Choose the **best** way to combine the ideas in sentences 14 and 15 into one sentence.

    The museum was a fun place. I learned a lot.

    a. The museum was a fun place learning a lot.
    b. A fun place where I learned a lot.
    c. Learned the museum was a fun place.
    d. The museum was a fun place where I learned a lot.

Ricardo's third-grade class is studying space. His teacher asked each student to choose one planet and to write about it. Ricardo chose Jupiter. He took notes at the library and wrote a rough draft. Now he needs your help to edit and revise his work.

Here is Ricardo's rough draft. Read it and then answer questions 1–11.

(1) Jupiter is the fifth planet, and Jupiter is four hundred and eighty million miles away from the sun. (2) It is mostly made of two gases, hydrogen and helium. (3) There is some sulfur, too. (4) The sulfur makes the planet look orange and yellow.

(5) Jupiter is the largest planet in our Solar System. (6) Twelfe Earths could fit in its diameter! (7) Jupiter is also the heavier planet. (8) It weighs a lot. (9) Jupiter is famous for its great red spot. (10) The spot is a huge spinning weather system. (11) A big hurricane, it looks like, I think. (12) A hurricane knocked down my tree house last year. (13) People have known about the red spot for three hundred years. (14) Maybe it is even older than that.

(15) Jupiter has sixteen moons, one of the moons, Io, has volcanoes. (16) I wish Earth will have sixteen moons. (17) The nights would be so beautiful!

1. Read sentence 11. It is poorly written.

   A big hurricane, it looks like, I think.

   Choose the **best** way to rewrite this sentence.

   a. A big hurricane, I think it looks like.
   b. Looking like a big hurricane, I think.
   c. A big hurricane. I think it looks like one.
   d. I think it looks like a big hurricane.

2. Choose the topic sentence for the paragraph that begins with sentence 5.

   f. Jupiter is famous for its great red spot.
   g. A big hurricane, it looks like, I think.
   h. A hurricane knocked down my tree house last year.
   j. It weighs a lot.

3. Read sentence 1. It is poorly written.

   Jupiter is the fifth planet, and Jupiter is four hundred and eighty million miles away from the sun.

   Choose the **best** way to rewrite the sentence so that it does not repeat ideas.

   a. Jupiter is four hundred and eighty million miles away from the sun.
   b. Jupiter, the fifth planet, is four hundred and eighty million miles away from the sun.
   c. Jupiter is the fifth planet far away from the sun.
   d. Jupiter is four hundred and eighty million miles away from the fifth planet.

4. Choose the correct way to write the underlined part of sentence 6.

   <u>Twelfe</u> **Earths could fit in its diameter!**

   f. Twelv
   g. Twelve
   h. Twelfth
   j. no change neeeded

5. Choose the correct way to write the underlined part of sentence 5.

   Jupiter is the largest planet in our <u>Solar System.</u>

   a. Solar system.
   b. solar System.
   c. solar system.
   d. no change neeeded

6. Choose the sentence that does **not** belong in the paragraph that begins with sentence 5.

    f. sentence 14
    g. sentence 12
    h. sentence 11
    j. sentence 13

7. Choose the correct way to write the underlined part of sentence 7.

Jupiter is also the <u>heavier</u> planet.

    a. most heavy
    b. heaviest
    c. heavy
    d. no change neeeded

8. Choose the correct way to write the underlined part of sentence 10.

The spot is <u>a huge spinning weather system.</u>

    f. a huge, spinning, weather system.
    g. a huge, spinning weather system.
    h. a huge spinning, weather system.
    j. no change neeeded

9. Read sentence 15. It is poorly written.

Jupiter has sixteen moons, one of the moons, Io, has volcanoes.

Choose the **best** way to rewrite this sentence.

a. Jupiter has sixteen moons that have volcanoes.
b. Jupiter has sixteen moon volcanoes.
c. Jupiter has sixteen volcanoes on the moon.
d. Jupiter has sixteen moons. One of the moons, Io, has volcanoes.

10. Choose the correct way to write the underlined part of sentence 16.

<u>I wish Earth will have</u> sixteen moons.

f. I wish Earth had
g. I wish Earth was having
h. I wish Earth will have had
j. no change neeeded

11. Ricardo wants to change sentence 8 so that it is more specific.

It weighs <u>a lot.</u>

Choose the **best** way to rewrite the underlined part of the sentence.

a. a heavy amount more than others.
b. a whole incredible lot.
c. more than all of the other planets put together.
d. tons.

Jonathan is in the third grade. His class is learning how to use the dictionary. He wanted to find out who wrote the first American English dictionary. Jonathan took notes at the library and put them into a graphic organizer. Then he wrote a rough draft of a report about Noah Webster. He needs your help editing and revising it.

Here is Jonathan's rough draft. Read it and then answer questions 1–11.

(1) Noah Webster is famous for writing the first American English dictionary. (2) He was born in <u>west Hartford, Connecticut,</u> in 1758. (3) He went to college at Yale. (4) Yale was the only college in Connecticut back then. (5) He finished school. (6) He <u>will become</u> a teacher.

(7) Noah <u>didnt'</u> like the schools in America. (8) Seventy kids had to sit in one room. (9) They had few supplies. (10) They had to use books from England. (11) Noah thought they should have American books. (12) I bought two books at a book fair yesterday.

(13) In 1806, Noah published the first American dictionary. (14) His best dictionary in 1828. (15) It was called *An American Dictionary of the English Language*. (16) He had to learn twenty-six languages to write it! (17) He wanted to know the <u>oragins</u> of all of the words. (18) There were tons of words in <u>him</u> dictionary!

1. Choose the **best** way to combine the ideas in sentences 5 and 6 into one sentence.

    He finished school. He <u>will become</u> a teacher.

    a. He finished being a teacher at school.
    b. He finished school teaching.
    c. He finished school and became a teacher.
    d. Finished school became a teacher.

118

2. Choose the correct way to write the underlined part of sentence 2.

   He was born in <u>west Hartford, Connecticut,</u> in 1758.

   f. west hartford, Connecticut,
   g. West hartford, Connecticut,
   h. West Hartford, Connecticut,
   j. No change is needed.

3. Choose the sentence that **best** fits right after sentence 9.

   a. The supplies they did have were in poor condition.
   b. The schoolhouse was beautiful.
   c. The weather was sunny and warm.
   d. The books were brand-new.

4. Choose the correct way to write the underlined part of sentence 6.

   He <u>will become</u> a teacher.

   f. would have become
   g. became
   h. was becoming
   j. No change is needed.

5. Choose the sentence that does **not** belong in the paragraph that begins with sentence 7.

   a. sentence 9
   b. sentence 8
   c. sentence 12
   d. sentence 11

119

6. Choose the correct way to write the underlined part of sentence 7.

   Noah <u>didnt'</u> like the schools in America.

   f. didt
   g. don't
   h. didn't
   j. No change is needed.

7. Which one of these is **not** a complete sentence?

   a. Noah Webster is famous for writing the first American English dictionary.
   b. Yale was the only college in Connecticut back then.
   c. Seventy kids had to sit in one room.
   d. His best dictionary in 1828.

8. Choose the correct way to write the underlined part of sentence 17.

   He wanted to know the <u>oragins</u> of all of the words.

   f. origins
   g. originals
   h. origines
   j. No change is needed.

9. Jonathan wants to change sentence 18 so that it is more specific.

   There were <u>tons of words</u> in him dictionary!

   Choose the **best** way to rewrite the underlined part of the sentence.

   a. a really huge number of words
   b. a lot of words
   c. seventy thousand words
   d. thousands of words

10. Choose the correct way to write the underlined part of sentence 18.

   There were tons of words in <u>him</u> dictionary!

   f. his
   g. our
   h. their
   j. No change is needed.

11. Choose the topic sentence for the paragraph that begins with sentence 13.

   a. In 1806, Noah published the first American dictionary.
   b. His best dictionary in 1828.
   c. It was called *An American Dictionary of the English Language*.
   d. He had to learn twenty-six languages to write it!

Dontrell is in the third grade. His class is learning how to write instructions. His teacher asked each student to write directions for making something. Dontrell chose to write about making a blueberry shake. He wrote his rough draft, and now he needs your help editing and revising it.

Here is Dontrell's rough draft. Read it and then answer questions 1–11.

(1) <u>I going to tell you</u> how to make a shake.

(2) First, get what you need. (3) You will need <u>an cup</u> of blueberries. (4) Frozen blueberries are okay if you don't have any fresh ones. (5) You will need a cup of vanilla ice cream, a cup of milk, and a blender.

(6) Scoop out one cup of ice cream. (7) Put it into the blender. (8) My cat likes ice cream. (9) Then pour in the milk. (10) If <u>they want</u> a super-thick shake, use less milk. (11) Put in the blueberries.

(12) Last time, I forgot <u>too put</u> the lid on the blender. (13) <u>Blueberry</u> shake went all over the place. (14) I made a big mess I had to clean it up. (15) Always remember to put on the lid!

(16) Turn on the blender. (17) Turn the blender on and let it run awhile. (18) Pour some into a glass. (19) Enjoy!

1. Choose the topic sentence for the paragraph that begins with sentence 2.

    a. First, get what you need.
    b. Frozen blueberries are okay if you don't have any fresh ones.
    c. You will need a cup of vanilla ice cream, a cup of milk, and a blender.
    d. You will need <u>an cup</u> of blueberries.

2. Choose the correct way to write the underlined part of sentence 1.

    <u>I going to tell you</u> how to make a shake.

    f. I was going to tell you
    g. I am going to tell you
    h. I will be going to tell you
    j. No change is needed.

3. Choose the sentence that does **not** belong in the paragraph that begins with sentence 6.

   a. sentence 9
   b. sentence 11
   c. sentence 8
   d. sentence 7

4. Choose the correct way to write the underlined part of sentence 10.

   If <u>they want</u> a super-thick shake, use less milk.

   f. you want
   g. he wants
   h. you wants
   j. No change is needed.

5. Choose the **best** way to combine the ideas in sentences 16 and 17 into one sentence.

   Turn on the blender. Turn the blender on and let it run awhile.

   a. Turn on the blender, turn on the blender and let it run awhile.
   b. Turn on the blender, turn it on and let it run awhile.
   c. Turn on the blender, turn the blender on and let it run awhile.
   d. Turn on the blender and let it run awhile.

6. Choose the correct way to write the underlined part of sentence 3.

   You will need <u>an cup</u> of blueberries.

   f. a cup
   g. the cup
   h. any cup
   j. No change is needed.

7. Read sentence 14. It is poorly written.

   I made a big mess I had to clean it up.

   Choose the **best** way to rewrite this sentence.

   a. I made a big mess cleaning it up.
   b. I made a big mess that I had to clean up.
   c. I made a big mess I cleaned it up.
   d. I made a big mess. I had to. I cleaned it up.

8. Choose the correct way to write the underlined part of sentence 12.

   Last time, I forgot <u>too put</u> the lid on the blender.

   f. also put
   g. to put
   h. two put
   j. No change is needed.

9. Choose the sentence that **best** fits right after sentence 18.

    a. A chilled glass is the best.
    b. Don't use chocolate milk.
    c. Strawberry ice cream works, too.
    d. Don't forget the lid.

10. Choose the correct way to write the underlined part of sentence 13.

    <u>Blueberry</u> shake went all over the place.

    f. blueberry
    g. blueBerry
    h. BlueBerry
    j. No change is needed.

11. Dontrell wants to change sentence 1 so that it is more specific.

    I going to tell you how to make <u>a shake.</u>

Choose the **best** way to rewrite the underlined part of the sentence.

    a. a blueberry shake.
    b. a cold blueberry shake.
    c. a frosty and delicious blueberry shake.
    d. an icy blue shake.

Julie is in the third grade. Her class is getting ready to visit the science center. The special exhibit is about animal eyes. Julie's teacher asked each student to write about how eyes work. Julie finished her rough draft, but now she needs help editing and revising it.

Here is Julie's rough draft. Read it and then answer questions 1–10.

(1) <u>Hear's how</u> you see. (2) You don't really see things. (3) You see the light that <u>bounses</u> off the things.

(4) First, light goes into the pupil. (5) The black spot in the middle. (6) The cornea covers it. (7) Next, light goes through the lens. (8) The lens turns the picture upside down, and then the picture goes onto the retina. (9) The retina is the back of your eye. (10) Then the eye turns the light into some signals. (11) The <u>signals goes</u> to your brain. (12) It reads the signals and you see.

(13) Some animals <u>doesn't</u> have true eyes. (14) They have eyespots instead. (15) They just see light and dark.

(16) Human eyes are only one inch wide we can see well. (17) <u>Vultures saw</u> even better than we can. (18) They can see a dead animal two and a half miles high.

1. Which one of these is **not** a complete sentence?
   a. You don't really see things.
   b. The black spot in the middle.
   c. It reads the signals and you see.
   d. They just see light and dark.

2. Choose the correct way to write the underlined part of sentence 1.

   Hear's how you see.

   f. Heres how
   g. Hears how
   h. Here's how
   j. No change is needed.

3. Julie wants to change sentence 10 so that it is more specific.

   Then the eye turns the light into <u>some signals.</u>

   Choose the **best** way to rewrite the underlined part of the sentence.

   a. good signals.
   b. some kind of signal.
   c. a certain kind of signal.
   d. electrical signals.

4. Choose the correct way to write the underlined part of sentence 3.

   You see the light that <u>bounses</u> off the things.

   f. bounces
   g. bounce
   h. bounse
   j. No change is needed.

5. Read sentence 16. It is poorly written.

   Human eyes are only one inch wide we can see well.

   Choose the **best** way to rewrite this sentence.

   a. Human eyes can see one inch wide very well.
   b. Only human eyes one inch wide can see well.
   c. Human eyes, they are only one inch wide, we can see well.
   d. Human eyes are only one inch wide, but we can see well.

6. Choose the correct way to write the underlined part of sentence 17.

   <u>Vultures saw</u> even better than we can.

   f. Vultures are seeing
   g. Vultures see
   h. Vultures will see
   j. No change is needed.

7. Julie wants to add this sentence to the paragraph that begins with sentence 13.

   For example, some worms have eyespots on their bodies.

   Where would the sentence **best** fit?

   a. right before sentence 13
   b. right after sentence 15
   c. right after sentence 13
   d. right after sentence 14

8. Choose the correct way to write the underlined part of sentence 13.

   Some animals <u>doesn't</u> have true eyes.

   f. doesnt
   g. dont
   h. don't
   j. No change is needed.

128

9. Read sentence 18. It is poorly written.

   They can see a dead animal two and a half miles high.

   Choose the **best** way to rewrite this sentence.

   a. A dead animal they can see two and a half miles high.
   b. Two and a half miles high, a dead animal can be seen by them.
   c. From a height of two and a half miles, they can see a dead animal.
   d. They can see two and a half miles high dead animal.

10. Choose the correct way to write the underlined part of sentence 11.

   The <u>signals goes</u> to your brain.

   f. signals went
   g. signals go
   h. signals going
   j. No change is needed.

Justin's third-grade class visited the Dinosaur Museum last week. His teacher asked the students to write about some things they learned during their day at the museum. Justin wrote a rough draft and now he needs your help editing and revising it.

Here is Justin's rough draft. Read it and then answer questions 1–10.

---

(1) Last <u>weak,</u> my class went to the Dinosaur Museum. (2) The Dinosaur Museum, an interesting place.

(3) The museum was shaped like a big dome. (4) It was built over a very large, flat rock. (5) A man found the rock by accident in 1966. (6) I like to climb rocks. (7) He was driving a bulldozer. (8) A state building was supposed to go there. (9) When they found the rock. (10) They decided to build a museum instead.

(11) The rock was covered with dinosaur tracks! (12) When I pressed buttons, lights lit up the tracks. (13) I saw which way each <u>Dinosaur</u> walked. (14) This was my favorite part of the museum.

(15) In the museum, I <u>will see</u> how this area looked two hundred million years ago. (16) This was the <u>begining</u> of the Jurassic period. (17) The Atlantic Ocean was brand new. (18) Dinosaurs called "sauropods" made tracks in our area. (19) Sauropods ate plants. (20) They had <u>small heads long necks and long tails.</u>

(21) I think a visit to the Dinosaur Museum should be you, too. (22) I think you would enjoy it!

---

1. Read sentence 2. It is poorly written.

   The Dinosaur Museum, an interesting place.

   Choose the **best** way to rewrite this sentence.

   a. The Dinosaur Museum. It was an interesting place.
   b. The Dinosaur Museum. Was an interesting place.
   c. An interesting place.
   d. It was an interesting place.

2. Choose the correct way to write the underlined part of sentence 1.

   Last <u>weak,</u> my class went to the Dinosaur Museum.

   f. wake,
   g. weke,
   h. week,
   j. No change is needed.

3. Choose the sentence that does **not** belong in the paragraph that begins with sentence 3.

   a. sentence 9
   b. sentence 6
   c. sentence 8
   d. sentence 7

4. Choose the correct way to write the underlined part of sentence 13.

   I saw which way each <u>Dinosaur</u> walked.

   f. dinosaur
   g. Dinosaurs
   h. dinosaurs
   j. No change is needed.

5. Which one of these is **not** a complete sentence?

   a. It was built over a very large, flat rock.
   b. When they found the rock.
   c. This was my favorite part of the museum.
   d. I think you would enjoy it!

6. Choose the correct way to write the underlined part of sentence 16.

   This was the <u>begining</u> of the Jurassic period.

   f. beginning
   g. beggining
   h. begginning
   j. No change is needed.

7. Justin wants to add this sentence to the paragraph that begins with sentence 15.

   That was long before there were any humans.

   Where would the sentence **best** fit?

   a. right after sentence 15
   b. right after sentence 17
   c. right after sentence 18
   d. right after sentence 19

8. Choose the correct way to write the underlined part of sentence 20.

   They had <u>small heads long necks and long tails.</u>

   f. small heads and long necks and long tails.
   g. small heads, long, necks, and long, tails.
   h. small heads, long necks, and long tails.
   j. No change is needed.

9. Read sentence 21. It is poorly written.

   I think a visit to the Dinosaur Museum should be you, too.

   Choose the **best** way to rewrite this sentence.

   a. I think a visit to the Dinosaur Museum should be done by you, too.
   b. I think you, too, should think about a visit to the Dinosaur Museum.
   c. I think that you should also visit the Dinosaur Museum.
   d. I think that the Dinosaur Museum should be visited by you, too.

10. Choose the correct way to write the underlined part of sentence 15.

    In the museum, I <u>will see</u> how this area looked two hundred million years ago.

    f. saw
    g. seen
    h. will see
    j. No change is needed.

Carlos is in the third grade. His class is getting ready to visit the train museum. His teacher asked each student to write a report about trains. Carlos loves trains. At home, he looked at one of his train books and took notes. Then, he wrote a rough draft. Now he needs your help to edit and revise his paper.

Here is Carlos's rough draft. Read it and then answer questions 1–11.

(1) <u>Their</u> are two main types of trains. (2) Some are freight trains, and some are passenger trains. (3) We have in the United States, both kinds.

(4) Freight trains haul things. (5) They carry just about anything. (6) They can carry <u>coal, food, lumber, and even animals.</u> (7) <u>They will have</u> special cars. (8) To carry different things. (9) Refrigerator cars keep things cold. (10) Tanker cars carry liquids. (11) Livestock cars carries animals. (12) Gondola cars are very strong they can carry heavy things. (13) Freight trains never carry passengers.

(14) Passenger trains carry people. (15) Some trains can take us for long rides. (16) They have dining cars. (17) They have sleeping cars. (18) Ferry boats carry cars. (19) <u>Comuter</u> trains are for people who ride to work every day. (20) My mother rides a train to work every day. (21) She is glad the train was invented!

1. Read sentence 3. It is poorly written.

   We have in the United States, both kinds.

   Choose the **best** way to rewrite this sentence.

   a. We have both kinds in the United States.
   b. We have them in the United States. Both kinds.
   c. We have both kinds. In the United States.
   d. Both kinds we have in the United States.

2. Choose the correct way to write the underlined part of sentence 1.

   <u>Their</u> are two main types of trains.

   f. They're
   g. There
   h. Thier
   j. No change is needed.

3. Which one of these is **not** a complete sentence?

   a. Some are freight trains, and some are passenger trains.
   b. To carry different things.
   c. Freight trains never carry passengers.
   d. They have dining cars.

4. Choose the correct way to write the underlined part of sentence 7.

   <u>They will have</u> special cars.

   f. They had
   g. They are having
   h. They have
   j. No change is needed.

5. Read sentence 12. It is poorly written.

   Gondola cars are very strong they can carry heavy things.

   Choose the **best** way to rewrite this sentence.

   a. Gondola cars are very strong and heavy.
   b. Gondola cars are very strong, and they can carry heavy things.
   c. Gondola cars carry strong, heavy things.
   d. Gondola cars are very strong. Carrying heavy things.

6. Choose the correct way to write sentence 11.

   Livestock cars carries animals.

   f. Livestocks car carry animals.
   g. Livestock car carry animals.
   h. Livestock cars carry animals.
   j. No change is needed.

7. Choose the **best** way to combine the ideas in sentences 16 and 17 into one sentence.

   They have dining cars. They have sleeping cars.

   a. They have dining cars and sleeping cars.
   b. They have dining cars, or they have sleeping cars.
   c. They have dining sleeping cars.
   d. They have different kinds of cars.

8. Choose the correct way to write the underlined part of sentence 6.

   They can carry <u>coal, food, lumber, and even animals.</u>

   f. coal, food, lumber, and, even, animals.
   g. coal, food and lumber and even animals.
   h. coal and food and lumber and even animals.
   j. No change is needed.

9. Choose the sentence that does **not** belong in the paragraph that begins with sentence 14.

   a. sentence 15
   b. sentence 14
   c. sentence 20
   d. sentence 18

10. Choose the correct way to write the underlined part of sentence 19.

<u>Comuter</u> trains are for people who ride to work every day.

   f. Commuter
   g. Computer
   h. Comutter
   j. No change is needed.

11. Carlos wants to change sentence 20 so that it is more specific.

My mother rides <u>a train</u> to work every day.

Choose the **best** way to rewrite the underlined part of the sentence.

   a. a nice train
   b. a commuter train
   c. a Railway Express commuter train
   d. some kind of special train

137

Martha is in the third grade. Her science class did an experiment, and her teacher asked each student to write a report about it. Martha took notes with her science partner. Then she wrote an outline. Now she is finished with her rough draft, but she needs your help editing and revising it.

Here is Martha's rough draft. Read it and then answer questions 1–11.

(1) We wanted to know what would happen when we dropped raisins into ginger ale. (2) First, we droped pennys into the bottle. (3) They sank to the bottom. (4) We thought sinking would be the raisins, too.

(5) We got a New Bottle of ginger ale. (6) We took five raisins. (7) We put them into the bottle. (8) They sank at first then bubbles started to stick to them. (9) The raisins floated up to the top. (10) After a minute, they floated back down. (11) They kept going up and down.

(12) There are one hundred pennies in a dollar. (13) The raisins were lighter then pennies. (14) They had wrinkles, so they held more bubbles. (15) When they got to the top, the bubbles broke. (16) Then the raisins sank back down. (17) So, raisins worked better than pennies.

(18) In conclushun, when you drop raisins into ginger ale, they sink. (19) Then they rise and sink and rise and sink for a while.

1. Read sentence 4. It is poorly written.

   We thought sinking would be the raisins, too.

   Choose the **best** way to rewrite this sentence.

   a. We thought, sinking to the bottom, the raisins would be.
   b. Sinking would be the raisins, too, we thought.
   c. We thought the raisins would sink, too.
   d. We thought the raisins too.

2. Choose the correct way to write the underlined part of sentence 2.

   First, <u>we droped pennys</u> into the bottle.

   f. we droped pennies
   g. we dropped pennies
   h. we dropped pennys
   j. No change is needed.

3. Choose the **best** way to combine the ideas in sentences 6 and 7 into one sentence.

   We took five raisins. <u>We put them</u> into the bottle.

   a. We took five raisins, then in the bottle.
   b. We put five raisins into the bottle.
   c. We put five raisins, we put them into the bottle.
   d. Five raisins were taken, and then they were put into the bottle.

4. Choose the correct way to write the underlined part of sentence 7.

   <u>We put them</u> into the bottle.

   f. They put them
   g. She put them
   h. They put us
   j. No change is needed.

5. Read sentence 8. It is poorly written.

   They sank at first then bubbles started to stick to them.

   Choose the **best** way to rewrite this sentence.

   a. They sank with the first bubbles that started to stick to them.
   b. They sank at first, then bubbles. They started to stick to them.
   c. They sank at first, but then bubbles started to stick to them.
   d. They sank at first, then bubbles started. Sticking to them.

6. Choose the correct way to write the underlined part of sentence 5.

   We got a <u>New Bottle</u> of ginger ale.

   f. new bottle
   g. New bottle
   h. new Bottle
   j. No change is needed.

7. Choose the sentence that does **not** belong in the paragraph that begins with sentence 12.

   a. sentence 15
   b. sentence 12
   c. sentence 14
   d. sentence 13

8. Choose the correct way to write the underlined part of sentence 18.

   In <u>conclushun,</u> when you drop raisins into ginger ale, they sink.

   f. concluson,
   g. conclucion,
   h. conclusion,
   j. No change is needed.

9. Choose the topic sentence for the paragraph that begins with sentence 12.

    a. There are one hundred pennies in a dollar.
    b. They had wrinkles, so they held more bubbles.
    c. When they got to the top, the bubbles broke.
    d. So, raisins worked better than pennies.

10. Choose the correct way to write the underlined part of sentence 13.

    The raisins were <u>lighter then pennies.</u>

    f. lighter than pennies.
    g. lighter pennies.
    h. light pennies.
    j. No change is needed.

11. Martha wants to change sentence 19 so that it is more specific.

    Then they rise and sink and rise and sink <u>for a while.</u>

    Choose the **best** way to rewrite the underlined part of the sentence.

    a. for a few minutes.
    b. for a hunk of time.
    c. for quite some time.
    d. until the ginger ale goes flat.

Lucas is in the third grade. His class just finished reading *Charlotte's Web*. His teacher asked each student to write a report about spiders. Lucas took notes from his spider book, organized them, and wrote his rough draft. Now he needs your help editing and revising it.

Here is Lucas's rough draft. Read it and then answer questions 1–10.

(1) Charlotte <u>is a orb spider.</u> (2) The kind that makes webs. (3) <u>Some spiders doesn't</u> make webs. (4) There are thirty thousand kinds of spiders. (5) They are all <u>arachnids</u>, and they are not insects. (6) Insects have wings and six legs. (7) Spiders have <u>eigt</u> legs and no wings.

(8) Orb spiders make silk webs. (9) The silk comes out like a liquid then it hardens. (10) The first part of the web is like the spokes on a wheel. (11) Bikes are better than wagons. (12) Spiders use non-sticky thread for that. (13) Then they start in the middle. (14) They make a central hub and then a free zone. (15) The spider can move around on the free zone. (16) Then comes the sticky part of the web.

(17) When a <u>bug lands</u> in the sticky part, it gets stuck. (18) The spider runs right over to the bug. (19) It wraps it up.

1. Which one of these is **not** a complete sentence?

   a. The kind that makes webs.
   b. Insects have wings and six legs.
   c. Then they start in the middle.
   d. It wraps it up.

2. Choose the correct way to write the underlined part of sentence 1.

   Charlotte <u>is a orb spider.</u>

   f. is orb spider.
   g. is an orb spider.
   h. is the orb spider.
   j. No change is needed.

142

3. Choose the topic sentence for the paragraph that begins with sentence 8.

    a. Orb spiders make silk webs.
    b. The silk comes out like a liquid then it hardens.
    c. Spiders use non-sticky thread for that.
    d. The spider can move around on the free zone.

4. Choose the correct way to write the underlined part of sentence 7.

   Spiders have <u>eigt</u> legs and no wings.

    f. ate
    g. eght
    h. eight
    j. No change is needed.

5. Read sentence 9. It is poorly written.

   The silk comes out like a liquid then it hardens.

   Choose the **best** way to rewrite this sentence.

    a. The silk comes out hard.
    b. The silk comes out like a liquid.
    c. The silk comes out like a liquid, and then it hardens.
    d. The silk comes out hard like a liquid.

6. Choose the correct way to write the underlined part of sentence 17.

   When a <u>bug lands</u> in the sticky part, it gets stuck.

    f. bug landed
    g. bug land
    h. bug is landing
    j. No change is needed.

7. Choose the sentence that does **not** belong in the paragraph that begins with sentence 8.

    a. sentence 13
    b. sentence 12
    c. sentence 11
    d. sentence 14

8. Choose the correct way to write the underlined part of sentence 3.

    <u>Some spiders doesn't</u> make webs.

    f. Some spiders don't
    g. Some spiders didn't
    h. Some spiders do not'
    j. No change is needed.

9. Choose the **best** way to combine the ideas in sentences 18 and 19 into one sentence.

    The spider runs right over to the bug. It wraps it up.

    a. The spider runs right over the bug and gets wrapped up.
    b. The spider runs right over to the bug and wraps it up.
    c. The spider runs right over to the wrapped-up bug.
    d. The spider runs right over and the bug wraps it up.

10. Lucas wants to add this sentence to the paragraph that begins with sentence 17.

Later, the spider will have a yummy meal.

Where would the sentence **best** fit?

f. right before sentence 17
g. right after sentence 17
h. right after sentence 18
j. right after sentence 19

(1) Harriet Tubman was a woman. (2) She was born in Maryland. (3) She escaped from slavery in 1849. (4) She went to underline philadelphia. (5) She went back to Maryland, she went back nineteen times to free other slaves. (6) She helped three hundred slaves, and she never got caught.

(7) Harriet Tubman used the "Underground Railroad." (8) It weren't a real railroad. (9) It was a group of black and white people who wanted too help the slaves. (10) They gave the slaves food to eat and places to hide.

(11) There are some other reasons that Harriet Tubman is famous. (12) She was a nurse and a spy for the Union Army during the civil War. (13) In the war, she helped free seven hundred and fifty more slaves. (14) She worked for womens rights. (15) Elderly and poor black people she made a home for.

1. Choose the **best** way to combine the ideas in sentences 3 and 4 into one sentence.

   She escaped from slavery in 1849. She went to philadelphia.

   a. In 1849, she escaped from slavery and went to Philadelphia.
   b. She escaped from slavery in 1849, she escaped and went to Philadelphia.
   c. In 1849, she escaped from slavery in Philadelphia.
   d. In Philadelphia, she escaped from slavery in 1849.

2. Choose the correct way to write the underlined part of sentence 4.

   She went to philadelphia.

   f. PhilaDelphia.
   g. Philadelphia.
   h. philaDelphia
   j. No change is needed.

3. Read sentence 5. It is poorly written.

   She went back to Maryland, she went back nineteen times to free other slaves.

   Choose the **best** way to rewrite this sentence.

   a. She went back to Maryland, she went back nineteen times. To free other slaves.
   b. She went back to Maryland. Nineteen times, for other slaves.
   c. She went back to Maryland nineteen times. To free other slaves.
   d. She went back to Maryland nineteen times to free other slaves.

4. Choose the correct way to write the underlined part of sentence 8.

   It <u>weren't</u> a real railroad.

   f. wasn't
   g. won't
   h. wouldn't
   j. No change is needed.

5. Amber wants to add this sentence to the paragraph that begins with sentence 7.

   It wasn't underground, either.

   Where would the sentence **best** fit?

   a. right after sentence 7
   b. right after sentence 8
   c. right after sentence 9
   d. right after sentence 10

6. Choose the correct way to write the underlined part of sentence 9.

   It was a group of black and white people who <u>wanted too help</u> the slaves.

   f. wanted two help
   g. wanted our help
   h. wanted to help
   j. No change is needed.

7. Choose the topic sentence for the paragraph that begins with sentence 11.

   a. There are some other reasons that Harriet Tubman is famous.
   b. Elderly and poor black people she made a home for.
   c. In the war, she helped free seven hundred and fifty more slaves.
   d. She worked for <u>womens rights.</u>

8. Choose the correct way to write the underlined part of sentence 12.

   She was a nurse and a spy for the Union Army during the <u>civil War.</u>

   f. Civil war.
   g. Civil War.
   h. civil war.
   j. No change is needed.

9. Read sentence 15. It is poorly written.

Elderly and poor black people she made a home for.

Choose the **best** way to rewrite this sentence.

a. Harriet Tubman, elderly and poor black people, made a home for them.
b. Elderly and poor black people made a home for her.
c. She made a home for elderly and poor black people.
d. Making a home for elderly and poor black people.

10. Choose the correct way to write the underlined part of sentence 14.

She worked for <u>womens rights.</u>

f. women's rights.
g. womens' rights.
h. woman's rights.
j. No change is needed.

11. Amber wants to change sentence 1 so that it is more specific.

Harriet Tubman was <u>a woman.</u>

Choose the **best** way to rewrite the underlined part of the sentence.

a. brave.
b. a nice woman.
c. a good woman.
d. a courageous woman.

Stephanie's third-grade class is learning how to write letters. Her teacher asked each student to write to a friend and describe his or her favorite hobby. Stephanie has written her rough draft, and now she needs your help editing and revising it.

Here is Stephanie's rough draft. Read it and then answer questions 1–11.

(1) dear Rockel,

(2) I <u>learnt</u> how to play chess when I was six years old. (3) It's a really fun game! (4) I like it so much.

(5) In the game of chess, there are some really interesting pieces. (6) <u>The king and queen</u> are the most important pieces on the board. (7) You attack the enemy king, if he cannot escape, you win! (8) Thit is called checkmate. (9) <u>The queen was</u> the most powerful piece in the game.

(10) The sneaky knights are my favorite pieces in the game. (11) <u>They move</u> in an L-shape. (12) They can jump over other pieces. (13) I like to use knights to attack enemy pieces. (14) Two or three pieces at once, the knight can attack.

(15) I think chess is fun because I like to think of new ways to attack. (16) I can use my mind to solve puzzles and get out of danger. (17) There are a millions of different ways to play a chess game.

(18) Do you know how to play chess? (19) Would you like to learn? (20) I go to my chess club every week. (21) If you want to play sometime, let me know!

(22) Your friend,

(23) Stephanie

1. Stephanie wants to add this sentence to the paragraph that begins with sentence 5.

   She can move as many spaces as she wants in any direction.

   Where would the sentence **best** fit?

   a. right after sentence 5
   b. right after sentence 7
   c. right after sentence 8
   d. right after sentence 9

2. Choose the correct way to write line 1, the opening of the letter.

   dear Rockel,

   f. dear rockel,
   g. Dear Rockel,
   h. Dear rockel,
   j. No change is needed.

3. Read sentence 7. It is poorly written.

   You attack the enemy king, if he cannot escape, you win!

   Choose the **best** way to rewrite this sentence.

   a. If you attack the enemy king and he cannot escape, you win!
   b. If you attack the enemy king and cannot escape, you win!
   c. You attack the enemy king if he cannot escape. You win!
   d. You attack the enemy king. If he cannot escape. You win!

4. Choose the correct way to write the underlined part of sentence 6.

   <u>The king and queen</u> are the most important pieces on the board.

   f. The King and Queen
   g. The King and queen
   h. The king and Queen
   j. No change is needed.

5. Choose the topic sentence for the paragraph that begins with sentence 10.

   a. The sneaky knights are my favorite pieces in the game.
   b. I like to use knights to attack enemy pieces.
   c. Two or three pieces at once, the knight can attack.
   d. They can jump over other pieces.

6. Choose the correct way to write the underlined part of sentence 9.

   <u>The queen was</u> the most powerful piece in the game.

   f. The queen will be
   g. The queen will have been
   h. The queen is
   j. No change is needed.

7. Choose the **best** way to combine the ideas in sentences 11 and 12 into one sentence.

   <u>They move</u> in an L-shape. They can jump over other pieces.

   a. They move in an L-shape, they can jump over other pieces.
   b. They move in an L-shape, jump over other pieces.
   c. They move in an L-shape like other pieces.
   d. They move in an L-shape, and they can jump over other pieces.

8. Choose the correct way to write the underlined part of sentence 11.

   <u>They move</u> in an L-shape.

   f. They moves
   g. They moving
   h. They had moved
   j. No change is needed.

9. Read sentence 14. It is poorly written.

   Two or three pieces at once, the knight can attack.

   Choose the **best** way to rewrite this sentence.

   a. Two or three pieces at once, the knight can attack.
   b. Two or three pieces at once. The knight can attack.
   c. The knight can attack two or three pieces. At once.
   d. The knight can attack two or three pieces at once.

10. Choose the correct way to write the underlined part of sentence 2.

    I <u>learnt</u> how to play chess when I was six years old.

    f. learned
    g. learnd
    h. learnted
    j. No change is needed.

11. Stephanie wants to change sentence 20 so that it is more specific.

    I go to my chess club <u>every week.</u>

    Choose the **best** way to rewrite the underlined part of the sentence.

    a. once a week.
    b. every weekend.
    c. every Saturday morning.
    d. often.

153

Asta is in the third grade. Her class is reading about ocean life. She wanted to learn more about manatees. She found a book at the library and took notes on what she found. Then she used the notes to write a rough draft of a report about manatees. She needs your help to edit and revise it.

Here is Asta's rough draft. Read it and then answer questions 1–11.

(1) The first time I saw a manatee, I was amazed. (2) What a huge and unusual animal!

(3) Manatees are very old creatures. (4) They were here sixty million years ago. (5) There were still dinosaurs back then! (6) Their <u>cousin's</u> were the Steller's sea cows. (7) In the cold water near Russia and Alaska. (8) About two hundred fifty years ago, <u>sailers</u> discovered them. (9) Hunters started <u>killing them for there fur</u> and meat. (10) Very fast they went extinct.

(11) Today, manatees are so big, that they are called "sea cows." (12) They can weigh up to three thousand five hundred pounds! (13) I wouldn't be afraid of a manatee, though. (14) They are very gentle. (15) They only eat plants.

(16) Manatees are mammals, so they have to breathe air just like we do. (17) They can hold their <u>breathe</u> for twenty minutes. (18) They usually don't wait that long. (19) They come up for air a lot.

(20) If you go to the aquarium, <u>you saw</u> the manatees. (21) Maybe you, too, will think they are amazing.

1. Choose the topic sentence for the paragraph that begins with sentence 3.

   a. Manatees are very old creatures.
   b. There were still dinosaurs back then!
   c. They were here sixty million years ago.
   d. Very fast they went extinct.

2. Choose the correct way to write the underlined part of sentence 9.

   Hunters started <u>killing them for there fur</u> and meat.

   f. killing them for their fur
   g. killing them for they're fur
   h. killing them for thier fur
   j. No change is needed.

3. Which one of these is **not** a complete sentence?

   a. What a huge and unusual animal!
   b. In the cold water near Russia and Alaska.
   c. I wouldn't be afraid of a manatee, though.
   d. Maybe you, too, will think they are amazing.

4. Choose the correct way to write the underlined part of sentence 8.

   About two hundred fifty years ago, <u>sailers</u> discovered them.

   f. salors
   g. sailars
   h. sailors
   j. No change is needed.

5. Read sentence 10. It is poorly written.

   Very fast they went extinct.

   Choose the **best** way to rewrite this sentence.

   a. Very fastly they went extinct.
   b. They went really fast extinct.
   c. They went extinct, and they went quick.
   d. They quickly went extinct.

6. Choose the correct way to write the underlined part of sentence 6.

   Their <u>cousin's</u> were the Steller's sea cows.

   f. cousins
   g. cousins'
   h. cousin
   j. No change is needed.

7. Choose the sentence that **best** fits right after sentence 11.

   a. They can grow to be thirteen feet long.
   b. Sailors used to think they were mermaids.
   c. They can see and hear very well.
   d. Sometimes they get hit by boats.

8. Choose the correct way to write the underlined part of sentence 20.

   If you go to the aquarium, <u>you saw</u> the manatees.

   f. you were seeing
   g. you will see
   h. you had seen
   j. No change is needed.

9. Choose the **best** way to combine the ideas in sentences 14 and 15 into one sentence.

They are very gentle. They only eat plants.

a. They eat very gentle plants.
b. Only very gentle plants eat them.
c. They are very gentle, and they only eat plants.
d. Eating only plants and being very gentle.

10. Choose the correct way to write the underlined part of sentence 17.

They can hold their <u>breathe</u> for twenty minutes.

f. breth
g. breath
h. breathing
j. No change is needed.

11. Asta wants to change sentence 19 to be more specific.

They come up for air <u>a lot.</u>

Choose the **best** way to rewrite the underlined part of the sentence.

a. quite a bit.
b. all the time.
c. often.
d. every five minutes.

Gary is in the third grade. His teacher asked each student to choose one game and to write the rules for playing it. Gary chose Four Square. His rough draft is done, but he needs your help editing and revising it.

Here is Gary's rough draft. Read it and then answer questions 1–9.

(1) Four Square is an old game. (2) I like this game because it's easy to learn, and I like this game because it's fun to play.

(3) You have to have four squares they make one big square and each of the smaller squares is eight feet wide. (4) One player stands in each square. (5) One is the King square. (6) Then there are the Prince the Count and the Peasant.

(7) The King went first. (8) He hits the ball. (9) It lands in somebody else's square. (10) If she lands in your square, you have to hit it. (11) If you miss, or if you hit it before it bounces, you go down one rank. (12) You also go down one rank for hitting out of bounds. (13) Trade places with the lower player.

(14) Some peeple play this game with hacky sacks. (15) Then it's called Hackball. (16) The only difference is that you don't bounce the hacky sack.

(17) You should try Four Square. (18) Its a lot of fun!

1. Choose the sentence that **best** fits after sentence 1.

   a. My father used to play a lot of games.
   b. My sister plays chess.
   c. My father taught it to me last year.
   d. I want to teach my neighbor how to play it.

2. Choose the correct way to write sentence 18.

   Its a lot of fun!

   f. Its' a lot of fun!
   g. It's a lot of fun!
   h. It a lot of fun!
   j. No change is needed.

3. Read sentence 2. It is poorly written.

   I like this game because it's easy to learn, and I like this game because it's fun to play.

   Choose the **best** way to rewrite this sentence.

   a. I like this game because it's easy to learn and fun to play.
   b. I like this game because it's easy and I like this game because it's fun.
   c. I like this game because it's easy to learn, and this game because it's fun to play.
   d. I like this game because it's easy to learn, and I like it because it's fun to play.

4. Choose the correct way to write the underlined part of sentence 14.

   Some <u>peeple</u> play this game with hacky sacks.

   f. peaple
   g. peopel
   h. people
   j. No change is needed.

5. Read sentence 3. It is poorly written.

   You have to have four squares they make one big square and each of the smaller squares is eight feet wide.

   Choose the **best** way to rewrite this sentence.

   a. You have to have four squares they make one big square. And each square is eight feet wide.
   b. You have to have four squares making one big square being eight feet wide.
   c. You have to have four squares, they make one big square, each square is eight feet wide.
   d. You have to have four squares that make one big square. Each of the smaller squares is eight feet wide.

6. Choose the correct way to write the underlined part of sentence 10.

   If she lands in your square, you have to hit it.

   f. If it lands
   g. If he lands
   h. If they lands
   j. No change is needed.

7. Choose the correct way to write the underlined part of sentence 6.

   Then there are the Prince the Count and the Peasant.

   a. the Prince, the Count, the Peasant.
   b. the Prince and the Count, the Peasant.
   c. the Prince, the Count, and the Peasant.
   d. No change is needed.

8. Choose the correct way to write the underlined part of sentence 7.

   The <u>King went first.</u>

   f. King will have gone first.
   g. King had first.
   h. King goes first.
   j. No change is needed.

9. Choose the **best** way to combine the ideas in sentences 8 and 9 into one sentence.

   He hits the ball. It lands in somebody else's square.

   a. Landing in somebody else's square, he hits the ball.
   b. He hits the ball into somebody else's square.
   c. He hits the ball, and he hits it landing into somebody else's square.
   d. He hits the ball, and the ball he hits lands in somebody else's square.

Destiny is in the third grade. Her teacher asked each student to write a report about a book that he or she read during the summer. Destiny chose *The Paper Bag Princess* by Robert Munsch. She wrote her rough draft, and now she needs your help editing and revising it.

Here is Destiny's rough draft. Read it and then answer questions 1–11.

(1) This summer I read *The Paper Bag Princess* by Robert Munsch. (2) It is a <u>funniest</u> story.

(3) Elizabeth is a princess, she is a princess who is going to marry Prince Ronald. (4) Elizabeth lives in a castle and wears nice stuff. (5) Then a dragon comes along and burns everything. (6) The dragon kidnaps the prince. (7) Elizabeth has to wear a paper bag that is all she has.

(8) Elizabeth goes to the dragon. (9) If it's true that he can burn down forests. (10) The dragon likes showing off. (11) He burns down a hundred forests. (12) Then she gets him <u>too fly</u> around the world. (13) The dragon <u>get really tired.</u> (14) Elizabeth is smart to trick the dragon.

(15) Elizabeth goes to <u>resque</u> Prince Ronald. (16) He is mad at her because she looks like a mess. (17) He doesn't even say, "Thank you." (18) Elizabeth decides not to marry him. (19) I think that is a good <u>decision.</u>

(20) I like this book because it has a surprise ending and it is happy. (21) Also, it makes me laugh.

1. Read sentence 3. It is poorly written.

    **Elizabeth is a princess, she is a princess who is going
    to marry Prince Ronald.**

    Choose the **best** way to rewrite this sentence.

    a. Elizabeth is a princess. She is a princess who is going to marry Prince Ronald.
    b. Elizabeth is a princess, being a princess who is going to marry Prince Ronald.
    c. Elizabeth is a princess, a princess who is going to marry Prince Ronald.
    d. Elizabeth is a princess who is going to marry Prince Ronald.

2. Choose the correct way to write the underlined part of sentence 15.

Elizabeth goes to <u>resque</u> Prince Ronald.

f. rescue
g. rescu
h. resqueue
j. No change is needed.

3. Destiny wants to change sentence 4 so that it is more specific.

Elizabeth lives in a castle and <u>wears nice stuff.</u>

Choose the **best** way to rewrite the underlined part of the sentence.

a. wears good stuff.
b. wears fancy clothes.
c. wears nice things.
d. wears a few things.

4. Choose the correct way to write the underlined part of sentence 2.

It is a <u>funniest</u> story.

f. funnier
g. very funny
h. more funny
j. No change is needed.

5. Choose the correct way to write the underlined part of sentence 13.

   The dragon <u>get really tired.</u>

   a. getting really tired.
   b. gotted really tired.
   c. gets really tired.
   d. No change is needed.

6. Read sentence 7. It is poorly written.

   Elizabeth has to wear a paper bag that is all she has.

   Choose the **best** way to rewrite this sentence.

   f. Elizabeth has to wear a paper bag because that is all she has.
   g. Elizabeth has to wear all she has.
   h. Elizabeth has to wear a paper bag that she has is all.
   j. Elizabeth has to wear a paper bag, all she has is a paper bag.

7. Which one of these is **not** a complete sentence?

   a. Elizabeth lives in a castle and wears nice stuff.
   b. Then a dragon comes along and burns everything.
   c. If it's true that he can burn down forests.
   d. Elizabeth is smart to trick the dragon.

8. Choose the correct way to write the underlined part of sentence 12.

   Then she gets him <u>too fly</u> around the world.

   f. two fly
   g. to fly
   h. two flies
   j. No change is needed.

9. Choose the topic sentence for the paragraph that begins with sentence 8.

    a. Elizabeth goes to the dragon.
    b. The dragon likes showing off.
    c. He burns down a hundred forests.
    d. Elizabeth is smart to trick the dragon.

10. Choose the correct way to write the underlined part of sentence 19.

    I think that is a good <u>decision.</u>

    f. desision.
    g. decicion.
    h. desishun.
    j. No change is needed.

11. Choose the sentence that **best** fits right after sentence 16.

    a. He complains about her clothes and hair.
    b. The dragon is mean.
    c. Elizabeth is a rich princess.
    d. The dragon has no fire.

NOTES

166

NOTES

NOTES

Made in the USA
Middletown, DE
30 May 2020